Heinemann History Scheme

INTO THE TWENTIETH CENTURY

FOUNDATION

BOOK 3

Judith Kidd

Rosemary Rees

Heinemann Educational Publishers
Halley Court, Jordan Hill, Oxford, OX2 8EJ
Part of Harcourt Education Limited

Heinemann is the registered trademark of
Harcourt Education Limited

© Judith Kidd and Rosemary Rees 2003

First published 2003

07 06 05 04 03
10 9 8 7 6 5 4 3 2 1

First published 2003

ISBN 0 435 32601 5

05 04 03
10 9 8 7 6 5 4 3 2 1

Designed and typeset by Visual Image, Taunton
This edition designed by Paul Davies and Associates
Original illustrations © Harcourt Education
Limited, 2002
Illustrated by Paul Bale, Ian Heard and Keith Richmond
Cover design by Hicks design
Printed in Italy by Trento S.r.l

Acknowledgements
Every effort has been made to contact copyright holders
of material reproduced in this book. Any ommisions
will be rectified in subsequent printings if notice is
given to the publishers.

Photographic acknowledgements
The authors and publishers would like to thank the
following for permission to reproduce photographs:

Associated Press: pp. 93, 98; Bridgeman Art Library: pp. 13, 58, 83,
195, 196 (top), 200, 204, 209, 229; Centre for the Study of Cartoons
and Caricature: pp. 123, 136 (top), 246; Corbis UK Ltd: pp. 33, 36
(bottom), 39, 102 (right), 206, 213, 218 (bottom); David King
Collection: p. 136 (bottom); Fortean Picture Library: p. 196
(bottom); Hiroshima Peace Memorial Museum: p. 121 (bottom right
and left); Hulton Getty: pp. 43, 55, 102 (both), 106, 152, 203; Image
Bank: p. 162; Imperial War Museum: pp. 77, 242; Katz Pictures:
p. 138; Kobal Collection: p. 161; Magnum/Danny Lyon: p. 36 (top);
Mansell Collection: pp.16, 32; Mary Evans Picture Library: pp. 12,
20, 23, 60, 116, 150, 158, 205 (top); Peter Newark's Military
Pictures: pp. 107, 113; Popperfoto: pp. 41 (top, middle, bottom
right), 95, 103 (bottom), 160, 168, 194, 217, 232, 234, 238; Punch:
pp. 78, 183; Tate Gallery: p. 47; Topham Picturepoint: pp. 41
(bottom left), 74, 81 (both), 88 (both), 103 (top), 104, 121 (top), 169,
212, 218 (top), 237, 245.

Cover photograph: © Imperial War Museum

Written source acknowledgements
The authors and publishers gratefully acknowledge the
following publications from which written sources in
the book are drawn. In some sources the wording or
sentence structure has been simplified.

G Alperovitz, *Atomic Diplomacy: Hiroshima and Potsdam*, Secker &
Warburg, 1966: p.216; V Brittain, *Testament of Youth*, Fontana, 1979:
p.76 M Chaikin, *A Nightmare in History*, Clarion, 1987: pp.153–4, 170;
J R Clynes, *Memoirs*, London, 1937: p.239 B Devlin, *The Price of My
Soul*, Deutsch, 1969: p.95; S Everett, *The History of Slavery*, Grange
Books, 1996: p.26; R Field, *African Peoples of the Americas*, Cambridge
University Press, 1995: p.29; A Frank, *The Diary of a Young Girl*,
Penguin, 2000: pp.163–5; G M Fraser, *Quartered Safe Out Here*, Harvill,
1992: p.167;P Gourevitch, *We Wish To Inform You That Tomorrow We
Will Be Killed With Our Families*, Picador, 1999: p.109; W Heyen, *Erika:
Poems of the Holocaust*, Time Being Press, 1991: p.173; D Hinds, *Black
Peoples of the Americas, 1500-1900s*, CollinsEducational, 1992: pp.30,
31, 34; A Hitler, *Mein Kampf*, Hutchinson, 1969: p.148; J & L Horton
(Eds), *History of African American People*, Salamander Books, 1995:
p.13; *The Independent*, article by Steve Crawshaw, 27 November 1999:
p.176; C Isaacman, *Pathways Through the Holocaust*, Ktav Publishing
House, 1988: pp.153, 158; Keesing, *Contemporary Archives*, Keesing's
Worldwide, 1989: p.138; T & S Lancaster, *Britain and the World: The
20th Century*, Causeway Press, 1992: p.170; Primo Levi, *If This Is A
Man (Survival In Aucshwitz)*, translated by Stuart Woolf, copyright ©
1959 by Orion Press, © 1958 by Giulio Einaudi editore S.P.A. Used by
permission of Viking Penguin, a division of Penguin Putnam Inc.; W K
Marshall (Ed.), *The Colthurst Journal*, KTO Press, 1977: p.20
K Martin, *Father Figures*, Penguin, 1969: p.246; E McCann, *War and
an Irish Town*, Penguin, 1974: p.92; *The New York Times*, January 1944:
p.167; E Ringelblum, *Notes from the Warsaw Ghetto*, McGraw-Hill,
1958: p.154; B Rogasky, *Smoke and Ashes*, Oxford University Press,
1988: p.155; S Rowbotham, *A Century of Women*, Penguin, 1999: p.77
J Scott, *Medicine Through Time*, Collins, 1990: p.210; L C B Seaman,
Post-Victorian Britain, London, 1966: p.241; B M Senior, *Jamaica by a
Retired Military Officer*, Negro University Press, 1969: p.20; J Simkin,
Contemporary Accounts of the Second World War, Tressell, 1984: p.215
N Smith, *Black Peoples of the Americas*, Oxford University Press, 1992:
pp.25, 30; *The Times*, 1968: p.93; V B Thompson, *The Making of the
African Diaspora*, Longman, 1987: p.21; M Weber, *Causes and
Consequences of the African American Civil Rights Movement*, Evans
Brothers, 1997: p.26; E. Wiesel, *Night*, trans. Stella Rodway, Penguin,
1981: p.173

"I Have A Dream", licence granted by the Heirs of Dr. Martin Luther
King, Jr., by permission of Intellectual Properties Management, Atlanta,
GA, ref – www.pbs.org/greatspeeches: p.39; Malcolm X's Audubon
address, © Dr Betty Shabazz, under licence authorised by Curtis
Management Group, Indianapolis, IA., ref – www.pbs.org/greatspeeches:
p.39; Richard Dimbleby transcripts of April 1945 taken from *BBC
History Magazine CD-Rom*, BBC Worldwide Limited: p.166; *Voices of the
Holocaust*, The British Library Board, published by The British Library
National Sound Archive, 1993: p.111

Contents

Unit 15: Black peoples of America – from slavery to equality?

You may not think your life is very free. You may moan about having to go to school or come home at a certain time. But we take 'freedom' for granted. This unit looks at a group of people that makes up a big part of America – African Americans. They fought for freedom from slavery. We will find out the answers to these questions:

- Where did most black Americans come from?
- How did they end up in America as slaves?
- How did they become free?
- How far are black people in America equal to white people?

WHAT DOES IT MEAN TO BE FREE? WHAT DOES IT MEAN TO BE A SLAVE?

We are used to thinking that people have rights. This means that we are treated fairly. We have laws to stop people or groups, like the government or the police, from having too much power. Some countries pass laws to make sure that people are free to make up their own minds about their lives. Black people in America had no rights at all.

SO HOW FREE ARE YOU?

In this country we can say, think and do what we like as long as we don't hurt other people.

Freedom can mean *free from* things as well as *free to do* what you like. Make a list of things you are free to do (like travel), then make a list of things you are free from (protected from).

Human rights groups stand up for the rights and freedoms of people. Some human rights groups think that even in this country we are not free enough. They say that inventions like CCTV (security cameras) stop people being totally free. Do you agree?

SLAVERY – A VERY OLD INVENTION

Slavery has existed for thousands of years. It was found in Ancient Egypt, China and under the Greek and Roman Empires. People became slaves for many reasons.

- They were prisoners of war.
- They were made slaves as a punishment.
- Their parents were slaves.
- They were sold with a plot of land.

Slaves in ancient times were white or black, Muslim or Christian.

A TRADE IN SLAVES STARTS

Slavery changed in the sixteenth century when a huge trade was started by the Spanish and the Portuguese. They wanted to take over land in **the Americas** to build up their **empires**. They needed workers to clear that land for them, so they went to Africa and bought black Africans as slaves.

SLAVERY CONTINUES

Here are some facts about slavery.

- Slavery was banned in the United States of America in 1865. It was banned in the British Empire in 1833.
- Many other countries carried on using slaves.
- Some countries still use slaves today.
- Human rights groups say that different types of slavery are used today. Two examples are child workers in India and child prostitution in Asia.

What does it mean?

The Americas
The Americas is the term used to sum up parts of north, south and central America, and the nearby islands. It is used to describe the time when no one country ruled this land and different countries were taking land for themselves.

Empires
An empire is a group of countries ruled over by one powerful country.

Question Time

1. Which of these phrases do you think match the word 'slavery'. Discuss your ideas in pairs or groups.

   hard work no wages no home

   no freedom no protection poor pay

2. Copy and finish this sentence to give your own explanation of the word slavery: *Slavery means ...*

3. Look up Amnesty International in an encyclopaedia or find its website. Name two countries where there is still slavery today. Try to find two facts about slavery in each country.

AFRICAN ROOTS – WHERE DID MOST BLACK AMERICANS ORIGINATE?

Most black Americans came from West Africa. West Africa is just one part of the huge continent of Africa. In the Middle Ages, West Africa was made up of many different groups, called kingdoms. Each kingdom had its own traditions and way of life.

- People in West Africa made their money from the gold mines, and from selling leather, ivory and copper.
- They traded with other kingdoms and with the Islamic Arabs who had taken over North Africa.
- The Arabs wanted gold in return for spices, salt, luxury goods and slaves.

> ### What does it mean?
> **Islamic Arabs**
> Arabs who were Muslims.

Activity Time

❶ Look at a modern map of Africa and the bottom map on page 7.

a How much bigger is Africa than Britain?
- 3 times?
- 50 times?
- 130 times?

b Where were the old kingdoms?
- Inland, or near the coast?
- On the west of Africa, or on the east?
- Close to trade routes, or very isolated?

❷ In the nineteenth century, many African countries were taken by European countries who wanted to build up their empires. These African countries became colonies of the European countries. In the twentieth century many of these colonies have become free to run themselves. Some of these modern African countries call themselves after old African kingdoms. Why do you think they have done this?

a Because the old names sounded good?
b Because the old names were original African names, not what Europeans had called them?
c Because they wanted to start again?

SOME EARLY WEST AFRICAN KINGDOMS

Ghana (fifth to eleventh century) – a very early kingdom.
This kingdom is not the same as the modern country called Ghana. It made money from gold, salt mines and farming. It was special because it was a large and developed kingdom, with a court and an army.

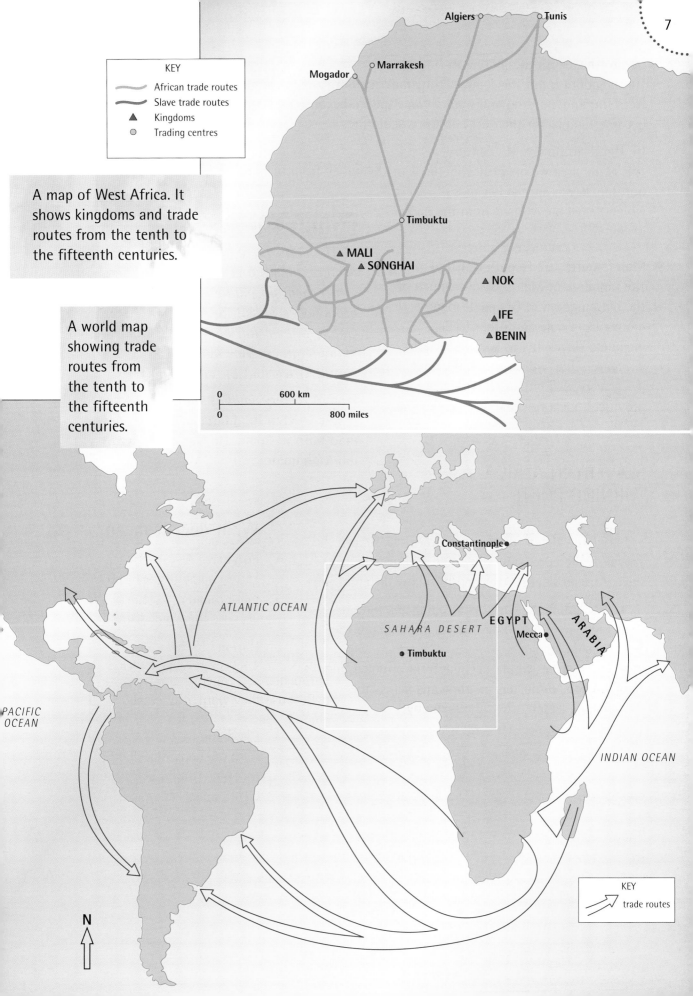

KEY

African trade routes
Slave trade routes
▲ Kingdoms
○ Trading centres

Algiers ○   Tunis ●
Marrakesh ○
Mogador ○

Timbuktu ○

▲ MALI
▲ SONGHAI
▲ NOK
▲ IFE
▲ BENIN

A map of West Africa. It shows kingdoms and trade routes from the tenth to the fifteenth centuries.

A world map showing trade routes from the tenth to the fifteenth centuries.

0   600 km
0   800 miles

ATLANTIC OCEAN

Constantinople ●

SAHARA DESERT   EGYPT
Timbuktu ●   Mecca ●   ARABIA

PACIFIC OCEAN

INDIAN OCEAN

N

KEY
→ trade routes

Benin (thirteenth to nineteenth century)
This kingdom is not the same as the modern country. It made money from farming, hunting and trade. It was special because its people became famous for their art and brass sculptures.

Ife (tenth to fourteenth century)
This is the area we now call Nigeria. It made money from farming and hunting. It was special because of its art, which its people learned from the people of Benin.

Mali (twelfth to fifteenth century)
The Kingdom of Mali took over much of the old Kingdom of Ghana. It made money from gold and other trade, including slaves. It was special because it was very big, with up to 400 cities.
It was very well organised with separate **provinces**, local rulers and tax collectors.

SLAVERY IN AFRICA: A TURNING POINT

Slavery had existed for centuries in Africa. Before the arrival of the Europeans you could still be sold as a slave. African slaves were used for many different jobs.

- Women might have been sold into a **harem**.
- Men were sold to be soldiers in India and the Muslim Empire.
- Other slaves would become farm or government workers, or porters on **caravans** across the Sahara Desert.

SOURCE 1

In Timbuktu there are many craft shops, doctors, judges and priests, and other clever men, all paid by the king. People bring books to sell for very high prices. Gao is a town full of very rich traders and many Negroes come here to buy cloth from North Africa and Europe.

From *A History and Description of Africa*. It was written in about 1526 by an Arab man born in Spain. He was called Hassan ibn Mohammed.

What does it mean?

Province
Part of a country, split up to make ruling it more easy. We also use the word 'district'.

Harem
A group of several wives or female servants who belonged to some rich Muslim leaders.

Caravans
A lot of people travelling together. Often they were traders.

HOW PEOPLE BECAME SLAVES IN EARLY AFRICA

- Prisoners were taken in wars between different kingdoms.
- People were kept as a punishment for a crime.
- Women and children were sold as slaves during a famine or drought to make sure that they were fed and stayed alive.

A famous African slave owner
- Mansa Kankan Musa ruled the Kingdom of Mali until he died in 1337.
- This kingdom was rich with gold mines. Musa used the gold to build up the capital city of Timbuktu with schools and palaces as well as mosques.
- Mansa Musa was a strict Muslim. He is famous for going on a pilgrimage to Mecca, the Muslim Holy City and to Cairo. The journey took over two years. He took over 8000 men with him. This included 500 slaves who all carried a gold staff to show off his wealth.
  He had over 100 camels carrying sacks of gold. He gave these as presents to rulers in Egypt.

SOURCE 1

The city (Jenne) is great and very wealthy. Traders come here and bring salt and gold. It is because of Jenne that so many caravans come to Timbuktu from every direction.

A description of the city of Jenne by Es-Saidi, a government worker who was born in Timbuktu in 1596.

SOURCE 2

They do no more work than any other person, even their master. Their food, homes and clothes are almost the same, although they are not allowed to eat with free men.

A member of the Benin people describing their slaves.

THE TREATMENT OF SLAVES

Different tribes treated slaves in different ways. Sometimes slaves were kept for a certain time – for example, four to seven years. Slaves could often work to buy their freedom. Children of slaves did not have to become slaves. When the religion of Islam spread in Africa the treatment of slaves improved. The Muslims believed that slaves should be treated well, properly fed and looked after when they were unwell.

Activity Time

1. What skills did people in West Africa have that might be useful to other kingdoms? Read pages 7 and 8 to help you.

2. Why did the armies think it was a good idea to keep some prisoners as slaves rather than send them home? Try to think of two sets of reasons for:
   a why it would be useful to keep prisoners, and
   b why prisoners should not be sent home.

3. Do you think that Mansa Musa took so many slaves on his long pilgrimage just to work for him? Explain your answer.

4. Copy a big version of this chart to collect evidence about slavery. Fill in the 'Before 1440' section now and the 'After 1440' later.

SLAVERY IN AFRICA	Before 1440	After 1440
Who were slaves sold to?		
Where would they work?		
How long were they slaves for?		
How were they treated?		

THE PORTUGUESE ARRIVE IN WEST AFRICA

During the fourteenth and fifteenth centuries, sailors from Europe began to explore new countries. They saw that they could use the new land and resources for themselves.

It was the Portuguese who first 'discovered' the West African coast in 1444. We should remember that this means 'discovering' it for Europe, because it was there already! The Portuguese sailors began to stop more often on the West Coast of Africa. They did not trade much at first. They just used Africa as a stop-over on the way to India and the **Orient**.

What does it mean?

The Orient
The countries of the east – especially East Asia.

THE 'DISCOVERY' OF THE AMERICAS

In the 1490s Portugal and Spain both began to claim land in the newly 'discovered' Americas. They competed with each other to increase the size of their **colonies**. To keep their new land safe and successful they needed workers.

Many **Native Americans** were killed at this time. Also, some were used as slaves. But more workers were needed, especially once gold and silver mines and **plantations** to grow sugar and tobacco had been set up. The demand for workers kept rising.

The Spanish and Portuguese began to capture African people and ship them to the Americas. The very first Africans in America were not really slaves at all. They were called indentured servants. This means they had their journey paid for. But in return they had to work for a certain number of years. When this time was up, they would be free.

Other European countries were quick to claim land in the Americas. They also needed workers so they began to trade in slaves. As sugar, cotton and tobacco became more popular in Europe, more slaves were needed. In 1619 the first black slave arrived in a British colony.

What does it mean?

Colony
An island or land that was ruled by another country.

Native Americans
People from tribes in North America. Sometimes called 'American Indians'.

Plantation
An area of land to grow sugar or cotton.

Ivory
Elephants tusks used to make trinkets and jewellery.

A TRADE IN LIVES

By the sixteenth century more and more workers were needed on the plantations in the Americas. So the slave trade also grew. Europeans stopped trading gold and **ivory**, and just traded in slaves. They set up forts on the West Coast of Africa where slaves were collected ready for the journey across the Atlantic Ocean. The Africans didn't have as much power or as many guns as the Europeans. So they could not stop the Europeans from taking lots of slaves.

SOURCE 3

This painting shows a 'barracoon' in Sierra Leone. This was a hut or type of prison where slaves were held before being shipped to the Americas. Slaves were often chained up by the neck or legs.

A NEW TYPE OF SLAVERY

So many men and women were needed as workers in the Americas that slaves would be slaves for life. Children of slaves became slaves at birth. There was no real escape, little chance of earning any money and no chance of return to Africa.

Question Time

❶ Look in an encyclopaedia or atlas. Find out which areas of Africa the European traders called:
a the Windward Coast
b the Ivory Coast
c the Gold Coast
d the Slave Coast.

❷ What do the names of these areas remind us about what the Europeans thought of West Africa?

CHANGING ATTITUDES

White traders began to change their attitudes towards
the slaves.

- **How?** Europeans began to think of the slaves as cargo.
  They thought the slaves were wild people who needed
  saving from their un-Christian lives in Africa.
- **Why?** Businessmen were making so much money on
  the plantations, they could afford to lose some slaves
  on the journey. There were plenty more available.
- **So what?** Now slaves had no rights and their
  treatment would get worse.

WHAT DID THE AFRICAN RULERS DO?

African rulers were in a difficult position. They could only
fight against the Europeans using guns. They could only get
guns by trading. The 'goods' that Europeans wanted were
slaves. Some African kings thought the only way to stop
their people being caught as slaves was to become the
slave catchers themselves.

SOURCE 4

*To take a black man
from the wilds of Africa
was a kind and Christian
task, because it changed
a wild and non-Christian
into a person who could
be improved by
Western countries.*

An extract from a 1950s
history book showing
attitudes towards slavery.

SOURCE 5

This painting is from 1833.
It shows a ship's captain
bargaining for slaves with
African slave dealers. The
place is Sierra Leone. The
slaves are being branded
(marked on their skin)
before they are put on
ships and sailed away.

Historians argue about the number of Africans taken across the Atlantic Ocean into slavery by the Europeans. One guess is that between 1490 and 1890, 15 million went to the Americas, and 40 million died on the journey.

There were so many slave traders and the slaves were treated as cargo, not as people. This makes it very hard for historians to know how many people were really involved.

THE EFFECTS OF SLAVERY ON AFRICA

- Some Africans became just slave traders and ignored crafts and farming.
- Europeans brought guns, alcohol and some new types of corn to Africa.
- The slave trade led to fighting between tribes as prisoners of war could be sold as slaves.

SOURCE 6

*The Africans damaged their own societies. They could make a profit by fighting to get slaves. After many wars over slaves, Africa became unstable. There was a lot of **famine** and the people were poor.*

Written by an historian of Africa in 1982.

What does it mean?

Famine
Hardly any food.

Question Time

1 Look at the 'barracoon' shown in Source 3. How might a man who ran the compound have shown off his slaves to a possible buyer? Choose from points **a** to **f** and explain why he would or would not have shown off these things.
a Slaves being whipped.
b Slaves being oiled to make their skin look healthy.
c Slaves working hard.
d Healthy slaves.
e Sick slaves being looked after.
f Slaves chained up in a neat row.

2 Find examples in Sources 3 and 5 which show that slaves were treated like animals.

3 Were there any positive effects of the slave trade on Africa? Explain your answer to the person sitting next to you.

SOLD INTO SLAVERY: WHAT WAS THE REALITY OF THE ATLANTIC SLAVE TRADE?

Remember that the first black Americans were not actually slaves. They worked as indentured servants for a fixed time. Some black people became free and settled in different parts of the Americas. Later slaves had no such chances of freedom.

THE TRIANGULAR TRADE

Many traders could see a way of making even more money, by turning the slave trade into a three-way trading system. They could make a profit on the cheap workers from Africa and sell goods from the plantations back in Europe. Sugar, cotton and tobacco were very popular. People would pay high prices for them. Many European countries joined in a three-way trading system. It was later called the Triangular Trade.

This map shows the 'Triangular Trade' route taken by slave ships.

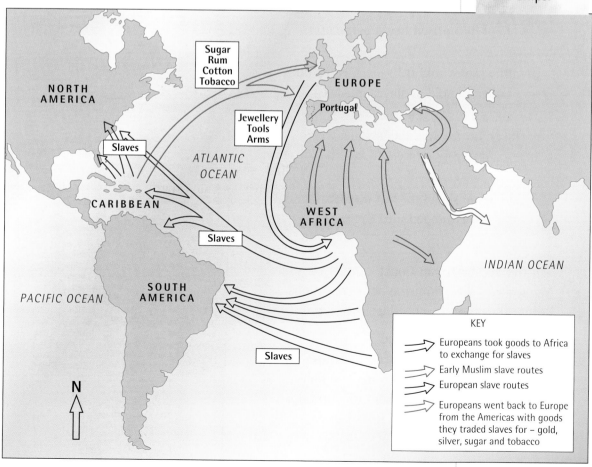

NORTH AMERICA

Sugar
Rum
Cotton
Tobacco

EUROPE

Portugal

Jewellery
Tools
Arms

Slaves

ATLANTIC OCEAN

CARIBBEAN

WEST AFRICA

Slaves

INDIAN OCEAN

PACIFIC OCEAN

SOUTH AMERICA

Slaves

N

KEY

Europeans took goods to Africa to exchange for slaves

Early Muslim slave routes

European slave routes

Europeans went back to Europe from the Americas with goods they traded slaves for – gold, silver, sugar and tobacco

The Triangular Trade was between Europe, Africa and the Americas.

- Ships loaded with European goods sailed to Africa. The goods were traded for African slaves.
- Slaves were taken to the Americas and sold to the settlers for a profit.
- With the profit, traders bought American goods to sell for even more profit back in Europe.

THE MIDDLE PASSAGE

The boat journey from Africa to the Americas was called the Middle Passage, because it was the middle stage of the triangle of trade. Here is how a slave might end up in the Americas.

Caught in Africa by a European trader
or an enemy kingdom

▼

Marched in chains to the coast

▼

Kept in a prison like a barracoon

▼

Healthy slaves sold to traders, weak ones
killed or sold as slaves in Africa

▼

Taken on the Middle Passage, which
lasted five to eight weeks

▼

Some slaves died of disease,
some jumped into the sea

On the West African Coast
Many slaves died from the poor conditions before they even got on the slave ship.

During the Middle Passage
- Many men and women were split up.
- Men were chained by the ankle in pairs.
- There was not enough room to stand up.
- The ships were dirty and full of disease.

SOURCE 1

This picture shows the space each slave had on a slave ship. The slaves are very cramped.

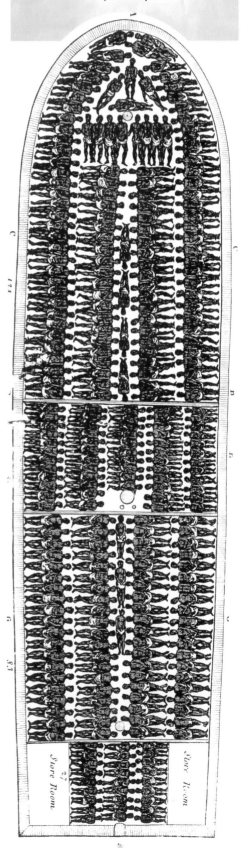

Question Time

1 Turn the Triangular Trade map on page 15 into a big triangular diagram. Label the following.
  a Europe, Africa and the Americas.
  b The types of goods that were traded.

2 Explain in a diagram or by finishing the sentences how each of these groups were kept happy from Triangular Trade.

  a *Plantation owners got ...*
  b *Slave traders got ...*
  c *Rich Europeans got ...*
  d *European craftsmen got ...*

3 Source 1 was used by people who disagreed with slavery. Why do you think that people against slavery chose this picture to make their point?

This map shows the areas where most slaves went to work. It also shows what work the slaves did in different areas.

NORTH AMERICA

Personal servants

Farming
Plantations
Servants

ATLANTIC OCEAN

CARIBBEAN

Plantations
Skilled workers
Servants

CENTRAL AND SOUTH AMERICA

PACIFIC OCEAN

Mining
Farming

ARRIVAL IN THE AMERICAS

Just before the slave ships arrived, sailors would clean the slaves up and rub oil into their skin to make them look healthy. Healthy slaves could be sold for a higher price. This is what happened when the slaves arrived at port.

- They were sold to plantation owners or to other traders.
- They were sold at auctions or at a 'scramble', which was a slave sale (see Source 2).
- Families were split up.
- Once they were bought, they had a number or mark burned on their skin, so people could see who owned them.

SOURCE 2

On a signal (the beat of a drum) the buyers rushed into the yard where the slaves were kept like sheep in a pen, and chose the ones they liked best. The noise and the rush increased the fear of the Africans. Family and friends were split up. Most of them never saw each other again.

Olaudah Equiano describes a 'scramble' in his story of his life. He wrote it in 1789. He had been taken from Africa and was sold in a scramble in the Americas. In a scramble, buyers grabbed as many slaves as they could.

Question Time

❶ List the types of jobs that slaves did when they arrived in the Americas. Look at the map on page 17 for the answers.

❷ What has the work of all slaves got in common?

❸ Think of two things that would probably have scared the slaves being sold at a scramble, like the one in Source 2. Write each one in a thought bubble.

HOW WERE SLAVES TREATED?

In the Americas, slaves made all the goods that their owners sold for a huge profit. But this did not mean that they were well treated.

In the Caribbean and the Southern States of America, plantation owners were very wealthy. There were also lots of slaves in Africa so they could be easily replaced. Remember that the slave owners thought of slaves as objects, not people. This meant the following things.

- Slave owners would often work a slave to death.
- Slave owners ruled very strictly to stop slaves from rebelling.
- Slaves could be killed or tortured as a punishment.

SOURCE 3

The whip used by the overseers (supervisors) on the cotton plantations is different from all other whips I have ever seen. The stick is about 20 inches (50 centimetres) long, with a large and heavy head. This is often filled with lead and wrapped in cat gut.

Charles Ball, who wrote this in 1836, was once a slave. He managed to escape.

Slaves had no rights

Slaves could not:

- marry
- earn a wage
- own property
- keep their own name
- give evidence in a court case against a white man
- worship in their own way
- learn to read and write
- refuse to do anything for their owner (including sexual acts).

Slaves with certain jobs or backgrounds became more important than slaves who only worked in the plantation fields. Some Europeans liked this, because it turned slaves against each other. So they would probably not rebel against the Europeans. The diagram below shows the different levels in slave societies, with the most important level first.

Different jobs	**Different backgrounds**
Slave drivers (bosses)	Mulattoes (mixed race, usually a slave mother and a white father)
Skilled slaves, e.g. carpenters	
Domestic servants	Slaves born in the Americas
Field workers	Slaves born in Africa

- Most slaves were treated badly by their owners and overseers (supervisors).
- A few slave owners made sure their slaves were well cared for, taught to read and write, and sometimes allowed to earn money to buy their freedom.
- Some white men who had children by slave women looked after their mixed-race children.
- Later, as the price of slaves went up, owners wanted to make the slaves live longer rather than work them to death.

SOURCE 4

This picture shows one slave being whipped by another.

Verdier 1849

SOURCE 5

Much money is made if a slave sells some goods, tobacco and corn, and by bringing up pigs and chickens.

From a book on Jamaica written by an army officer in 1835. Some slaves were given the chance to earn money, but their wages might be stolen by their owner.

SOURCE 6

The worst evil of slavery is the treatment of females. They are forced to be prostitutes, to work as hard as men and to breed more slaves whenever their masters want.

From the diary of Major J B Colthurst, published in 1847. He was a special judge sent to the Caribbean from Britain.

Question Time

1. What evidence is there in Source 4 of the following?
   a Harsh treatment of slaves.
   b Some slaves being treated better than others.
   c What some slave owners thought of their slaves.

2. Finish this sentence:
   This painting seems unreal because ...

3. Read Source 5.
   a What could some slaves do to get a better life?
   b What could stop them from getting a better life?

4. Prepare an answer for either Question a or Question b. Make a note of the key words, but give your answer in full spoken sentences.
   a Did slaves suffer mentally (in their mind) as well as physically (in their body)?
   b Did female slaves suffer more than male slaves?

5. Look back to the chart you started on page 10. Fill in the 'After 1440' column with as many points as you can. Use pages 18–20 to help you.

SOURCE 7

The slave may be 'used up' in seven years. A slave can be used as a breeder, as a prostitute, to serve drink and to practise surgery on. But the law says that slaves may not be used as a clerk (an accountant or assistant).

William Goodell writing in 1854 about American slavery.

FREEDOM: HOW WAS IT ACHIEVED?

Some slaves managed to fight against slavery and become free. They tried to beat slavery by:

- working slowly
- deliberately damaging crops
- rebelling against the people in charge of them.

Here is the story of some people who managed to beat the system of slavery.

What does it mean?

Safe houses
Places where people in danger could go. There they would be protected.

WHAT WAS THE UNDERGROUND RAILROAD?

The Underground Railroad was not a real railway. It was the name given to the system that helped slaves escape to the Northern States of America, where slaves were free. It was started in 1787 by Isaac Hopper, who was a religious man. He was also against slavery. He began to organise **safe houses** for escaped slaves to hide in. He gave slaves contacts to help them travel to the Northern States.

Up to 50,000 slaves escaped on the Underground Railroad. Escaped slaves, free black people and white people worked on the railway. Some people were 'conductors', who would risk their own lives to lead the slaves to freedom.

HARRIET TUBMAN (1820–1913) – AN ESCAPED SLAVE WHO RISKED HER LIFE FOR OTHERS

- Harriet Tubman escaped from slavery in Maryland, when her owner died. She was 29.
- She made 19 trips as a conductor for the Underground Railroad and saved 300 slaves.
- Slaves were hidden in carts with false bottoms and driven between 'stations' at night.
- Slave owners offered a reward for Harriet's capture. But she was never caught.

TOUSSAINT L'OUVERTURE IN HAITI – FROM REBEL SLAVE TO GOVERNOR

Toussaint L'Ouverture was born in 1743. He was the grandson of an African king. He lived in Saint Domingue, which became known as Haiti. Unusually, he was taught to read and write by his 'godfather'. He also studied Latin, geometry and french. He was then put in charge of all the other slaves on the plantation. Toussaint planned a slave rebellion with 3000 rebels. He beat the French rulers and became Governor of Saint Domingue in 1798. Toussaint led the only group to beat slave owners. The French took back Saint Domingue in 1801. Toussaint died in a French prison in 1804.

SOURCE 1

The journey was so hard over the rough mountain tracks, that often the men who went with her would give up. With sore, bleeding feet they would drop on the ground, groaning that they could not take another step. They would lie there and die. Or if their strength came back, they would turn back. Then brave Harriet would take out a gun. While pointing it at their heads she would say, 'Dead niggers tell no tales. You go on or die!'

From *Harriet Tubman – The Moses of her People,* by Sarah Bradford, 1886.

What does it mean?

Godfather
An older slave who kept an eye on younger slaves who had no family.

REBELLION ON BOARD THE *AMISTAD*

In 1839 the slaves on one Spanish slave ship, called the *Amistad*, revolted (rebelled). They were led by a man called Cinque. They killed the captain and the cook. Then they put the rest of the crew in a small boat. They tried to force the Spanish traders to go back to Africa. The ship was seen by the American navy. The navy rescued the Spanish traders and arrested Cinque and the rest of the escaped slaves. Cinque and the slaves were taken to court and charged with murder.

THE COURT CASE

The case of Cinque and the Africans (the slaves) was not a simple one.

- **The Africans**. They said they were not slaves, but free Africans because they had escaped.
- **The Spanish**. The Queen of Spain wanted the ship and all the slaves handed back to Spain.
- **The Verdict**. The jury and the highest court in America (the Supreme Court) agreed with the Africans. They won and went back to Africa in 1841.

SOURCE 2

A picture of Toussaint L'Ouverture drawn while he was alive.

Question Time

1 Look at pages 22–3.
   a Which of these people has risked the most to help slaves?
   b Which of these people has done the most to free black Africans?
   Give reasons for your answers to these questions.

2 Search in an encyclopaedia or on the Internet for either Olaudah Equiano (see page 18) or Henry Brown. Make a spider diagram of at least five facts about the person. Use key words and not full sentences.

THE SLAVERY DEBATE – WHAT DID PEOPLE THINK?

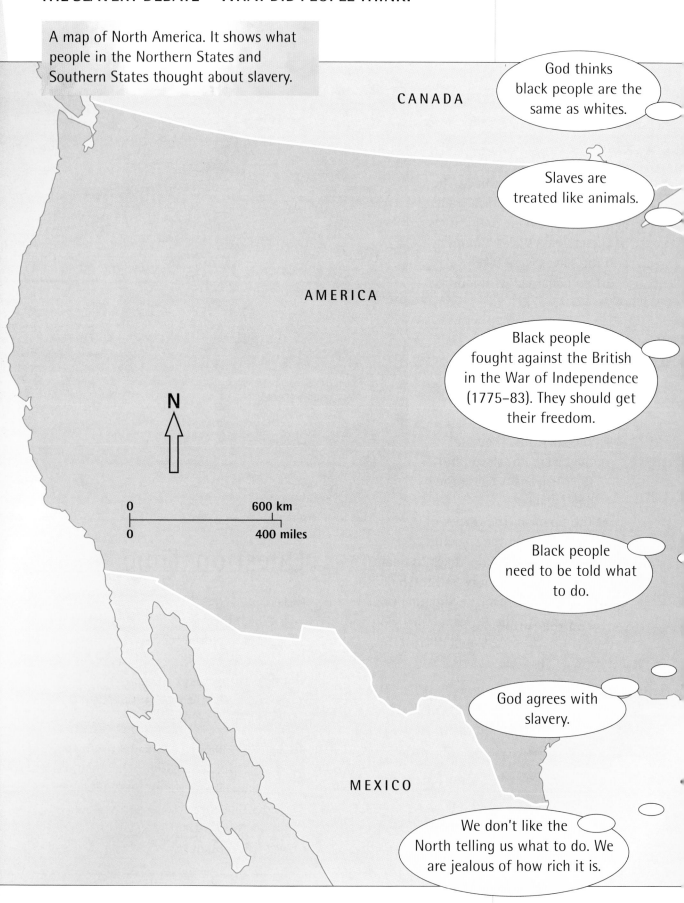

A map of North America. It shows what people in the Northern States and Southern States thought about slavery.

ATTITUDES TOWARDS SLAVERY

In 1776 the Declaration of Independence promised that American people would be free. But by 1861 the number of slaves increased from 700,000 to four million. Slavery became one of the causes of civil war in America, when the North fought against the South. Most of the North wanted to ban slavery. The South wanted to keep slavery.

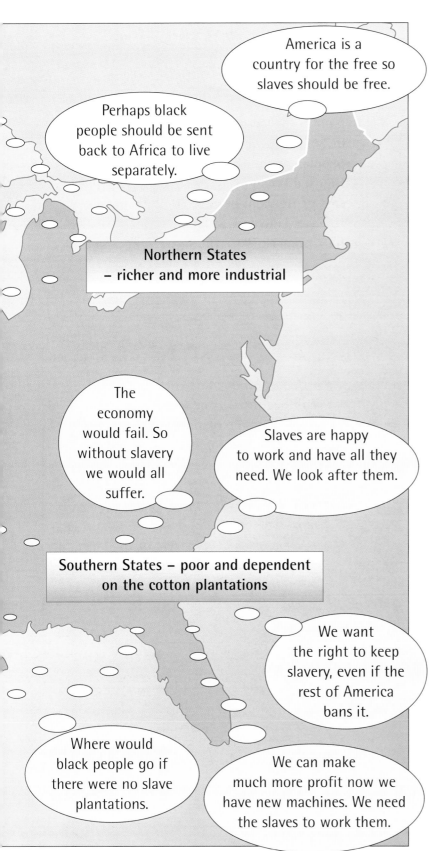

America is a country for the free so slaves should be free.

Perhaps black people should be sent back to Africa to live separately.

Northern States – richer and more industrial

The economy would fail. So without slavery we would all suffer.

Slaves are happy to work and have all they need. We look after them.

Southern States – poor and dependent on the cotton plantations

We want the right to keep slavery, even if the rest of America bans it.

Where would black people go if there were no slave plantations.

We can make much more profit now we have new machines. We need the slaves to work them.

SOURCE 3

What, to the American slave, is your fourth of July? It only reminds him of the unfairness and cruelty he suffers from. To him your celebration is false. Your shouts of freedom and equality are an empty joke.

From a speech made by Frederick Douglass at a Fourth of July celebration in 1852 (the day America became independent). Douglass was an ex-slave. He fought against slavery.

SOURCE 4

When Harriet Beecher Stowe published a novel giving an unpleasant picture of Southern slavery, Southerners strongly defended slavery. Fourteen novels supporting slavery were written in three years. Some writers wrote about how badly factory workers in the Northern States and in Britain were treated compared to slaves.

Adapted from Suzanne Everett's *T e History of Slavery*, published in 1996.

SOURCE 5

I have never wanted to make black people equal to white people in society and in politics. But a black person should be able to eat bread without asking permission, paid for with the money he earns.

From a speech made by Abraham Lincoln in 1858. Lincoln did not mean that black people should only be free to eat bread. He used bread as a symbol to show what sort of freedom he wanted black people to have. Lincoln was later President of the USA from 1861 to 1865.

Question Time

1 Write a newspaper report on a meeting of people living in a Southern State of America. The meeting was about whether or not to ban slavery in the State.
The people at the meeting were:
a plantation owners
b freed slaves wanting to stay in the South
c Church groups
d a black anti-slavery group
e a white anti-slavery group.
A vote to decide about slavery in the State was taken at the end of the meeting.
Now write your report. Use these sentence starters to help you. (You will need to put the sentences in the correct order.)

Remember to use pages 24–5 for ideas.
• *At the end of the meeting everyone voted on what to do. The result was …*
• *A meeting was held yesterday to …*
• *The question of slavery is a big one in this State. People are so upset about it because …*
• *The local Church leader said …*
• *The people who agreed with slavery the most were …*
• *Some black people were at the meeting. Their leader made two points …*
• *Another interesting point was made by …*

AMERICA DIVIDED

From 1777 to 1858, 19 Northern States banned slavery. Southern States wanted to keep slavery and did not want the central (called Federal) government to tell them what to do. The North and the South couldn't agree. They began to move further apart.

HE DRED SCOTT CASE

me black people went to court to try to win freedom by
w. One of the most famous court cases was held in 1857.
shows how America became split in two over slavery.

ed Scott was a slave who had moved around America
th his family as their master moved homes. Scott saved
ough money to buy his freedom. But his master wouldn't
cept it. Scott used the money to take his master to court.

hat happened in the court case

- Scott said that living in states that did not allow
  slavery made him and his family free.
- His master said he still owned Scott, wherever he was.
- The local court agreed with Scott. The State court
  agreed with his master.
- Scott appealed to the Supreme Court, which turned
  him down. The Supreme Court said black people were
  not totally equal to whites and that it was illegal to
  take away slaves from their owners.
- This meant that slavery could not really be banned
  and slave owners could take their slaves with them
  into free states. Black people had no rights.

Timeline of events that increased
divisions between North and South.

1776–1781 Slaves who agreed to fight on the British side in the War of Independence were freed.

1787–1804 The North began to ban slavery.

1820 Missouri Compromise (an agreement for both sides) drew a line between South and North on the map. Southern States could keep slaves.

1854 States could make their own decisions about slavery.

1857 Dred Scott said that black people had no rights.

1860 The new President of the USA, Abraham Lincoln, was a Republican. The South thought that all Republicans were anti-slavery.

November 1860 The 11 Southern States broke away from the North. They called themselves the Confederate States of America.

Question Time

❶ Finish these sentences.
  - *After the Dred Scott court case, slave owners could ...*
  - *Slaves could not ...*

❷ Choose two of the events from the
  timeline. Give one reason for each to
  show how they would upset the North or
  the South.

WAS THE CIVIL WAR FOUGHT TO FREE THE SLAVES?

In April 1861 the North invaded the South. It wanted to force 11 Confederate (Southern) states back into the Union (the USA). The civil war between North and South lasted until March 1865. Five days later President Lincoln was assassinated. The war was a struggle between Southern plantation owners and Northern businessmen. But slavery was not the only cause of the war.

Southern States' rights
- The South was worried by the power of the new Republican Party.
- The South wanted to pass their own laws.
- They wanted to keep taxes low.
- They also wanted to be able to keep slaves.
- They wanted Southern States to make their own decisions.

Save America
President Lincoln's main aim was to keep America as one country. He would even have allowed slavery if this had kept North and South together. During the war he needed men to fight for the North, so he began to push for freeing the slaves.

SOURCE 6

We do not say that the North is fighting just for black man's rights. But if we help them we can help ourselves.

Written by the editors of the Anglo-African newspaper published in New York.

Money problems

- Southerners did not like the taxes they had to pay.
- They thought that the Northern businessmen got a better deal from the government.
- North and South wanted different decisions made about how to run the economy of America.

Anti-slavery groups

The movement to ban slavery was getting popular in the North. In 1832 The Anti-Slavery Society was set up with black and white members. Other countries banned slavery, which helped the protests in America. Northern businessmen supported the groups because they wanted freed slaves to work as free men in their factories.

SOURCE 7

My main aim is to save the Union. If I could save the Union without freeing any slave I would do it. If I could save the Union by freeing all slaves I would do it.

President Lincoln speaking in 1862.

SOURCE 8

The iron gate of our prison stands half open. One rush for the North will push it wide open, and four million of our brothers and sisters will march out into freedom.

Frederick Douglass wrote this in a newspaper article to get black people to join the Union (Northern) army in 1863.

SOURCE 9

Our Confederacy (the Southern States) is founded on the great truth that slavery is normal for a black person.

Alexander Stephens, a Confederate (Southern) leader, said this in a speech in 1861.

THE IMPORTANCE OF BLACK SOLDIERS

In 1863 the **Emancipation Proclamation** was made. This was a statement that said slaves would be freed if they joined the Union (Northern) army. Ten per cent of the Union army was made up of black soldiers. So the war itself helped some black slaves become free. The Northern army treated black soldiers differently. They were paid, but they fought in separate regiments. The Southern army would not let any black men fight. They realised that this was a mistake just before they lost the war.

Question Time

❶ Give one way that fighting in the Civil War helped black people in America.

❷ Was the Civil War fought only to free the slaves? Answer in full sentences and paragraphs if you can. Use the paragraph starts below if you like. But you will have to put them into the correct order first.

• *Slavery was not the only cause, because the war was also about ...*
• *The result of war was ...*
• *The result for slaves was ...*
• *The American Civil War was fought between ...*
• *Slavery was one reason that the war was fought ...*

❸ Look at Source 8. The writer is not talking about a real prison here. What do you think he is talking about?

What does it mean?

Emancipation
Freedom.

Proclamation
An official announcement.

FROM EMANCIPATION TO SEGREGATION: HOW FREE WERE BLACK PEOPLE?

The fourteenth and fifteenth **Amendments** to the American **Constitution** in 1870 gave black people hope. They now had equal civil rights and the right to vote, legally own land, and marry and raise a family without fear of being split up.

The 80 years after the American Civil War brought many problems for poor people, white and black. Many states, especially in the South, ignored the law. Black people were still treated unfairly.

SHARECROPPING

Sharecropping was the system that the Southern landowners used after their slaves had been freed by law. The plantations were still owned by the same people as before, and people were still needed to work on the land. The freed slaves needed work. Sharecropping is when landowners gave one-third of their crops to the workers instead of wages. The workers could sell these crops and make some money. They had to wait for harvest to do this. They often had to borrow money until the crops were sold. Freedom did not seem that different to life before the Civil War.

THE FREEDMEN'S BUREAU

The Freedmen's Bureau was started in 1865 by the government. The Bureau dealt with any problems that freed slaves might have. It set up some schools and health care clinics. More black people were taught to read and write. But only 20 per cent were literate (could read and write) by 1874. Many Southern States made black people pass a literacy test before they could vote. White people did not have to sit the test. The Freedmen's Bureau only gave a little help to the freed slaves.

SOURCE 1

Ol miss and massa (master) was not mean to us at all until after the surrender and we were freed. They got mad at us because we were free and they let us go without a crumb of anything. We wandered around for a long time. Then they hired us to work and man, we've had a hard time then and I've been having a hard time ever since.

Frank Filkes, an ex-slave, wrote this in the 1930s.

What does it mean?

Amendment
When the Constitution is changed or updated.

Constitution
A list of basic ideas by which a country is run.

JIM CROW LAWS BRING SEGREGATION

Many Southern States felt the ban on slavery had been forced on them. Between 1890 and 1910 they passed their own laws, which forced black people to live separately from white people. This was called segregation. The laws were called 'Jim Crow', after an old plantation song.

Jim Crow laws forced black people to use separate hotels, transport, churches, schools and hospitals. This meant that black people were treated as second-class citizens. Violence was also used to scare black people away from voting and leading free lives.

MARCUS GARVEY'S PLANS FOR LIBERIA

What do you think of the man in Source 2? Look at his medals, his uniform and the look on his face. He is Marcus Garvey.

- Garvey was born in Jamaica. He set up the African Universal Negro Improvement Association in 1914.
- He believed in the idea of 'black nationalism'. This means that black people should be proud of their race and their African roots.
- He wanted black people from America to move to an African country called Liberia.
- Garvey eventually went to jail for fraud.
- Many of his ideas and his sayings, such as 'Black is Beautiful', were used by black campaigners in later years.

THE KU KLUX KLAN

The Klu Klux Klan (KKK) was started in 1865. It was a secret society of white people. The KKK believed that black people were inferior. They wanted to make sure that black people had no say. The KKK used brutal force, including lynching, against black people in the Southern States. Lynching is killing someone who may not even have committed a crime.

SOURCE 2

Marcus Garvey stood for hope for many black people.

The KKK was banned in 1872. But it became popular again several times afterwards. In the 1920s, the KKK had over five million members. They were famous for dressing in white robes and hoods so no one knew who was a member. Even some judges and policemen were members of the KKK.

Many black people wanted to get better jobs. They wanted to leave behind the **discrimination** they faced all the time. Many black people **migrated** North to the big cities. They often got jobs but had to live in the worst areas. These areas were usually slums, called ghettos. This meant they also had poor health care and schools.

What does it mean?

Discrimination
To treat someone unfairly.

Migrated
Moved to another place.

SOURCE 3

This photograph was taken in 1940. It shows KKK members at a ceremony.

THE TWO WORLD WARS

Black soldiers fought in both world wars. They had to join separate units to white men in the First World War. In the Second World War, some black men were trained to be pilots but they still could not join the marines or be an officer in the Navy. Fewer than 1 per cent of black soldiers became officers.

The two world wars gave new jobs to people in America, including black people. This is because there were so many people involved in the fighting, more black people moved to the North to work in the factories.

Question Time

❶ Why did many black people want to go back to Africa, as Marcus Garvey suggested?

❷ List two reasons why it was so hard to put an end to the KKK.

When white soldiers returned from war and wanted their jobs back, black people often lost their jobs. When white soldiers were treated like heroes, some black soldiers were attacked. This shows the problems that black people still faced.

CIVIL RIGHTS AND SELF-HELP ORGANISATIONS

Several groups were started to improve the rights of black people. They helped to make the government and the public aware of the problems.

- The Niagara Movement (set up in 1905) became the National Association for the Advancement of Coloured People (NAACP) in 1910.
- The National Urban League (NUL) worked to help black people who had moved to the cities.
- Churches were also powerful groups against segregation.

Black people sometimes disagreed about the best way to improve their rights. Two leaders in particular had different ideas.

- Booker T Washington set up a college to give black people basic skills, like carpentry. He thought that by peacefully improving black people's lives, they would slowly get more power and equality.
- W.E.B. Du Bois helped to set up the NAACP. He argued that black people needed **civil rights** first. Only then would they get more power and equality.

What does it mean?

Civil Rights
The rights of all people to equality and freedom in society and politics.

Question Time

❶ Search in an encyclopaedia or on the Internet for one of these topics.

- Harlem in the 1920s and 30s.
- Ella Fitzgerald
- Duke Ellington
- W.E.B. Du Bois
- Booker T Washington

a Make a spider diagram of some key words or phrases about your topic.
b Tell the rest of your group what you find out.

SOURCE 4

The negro (black) race in America needs help and is given problems. It needs protection and is given violence. It needs justice and is given charity. It needs leadership and is given apologies. It needs bread and is given a stone. The nation will never stand fairly before God until these things are changed.

From a statement given by the Niagara Movement in 1905.

Activity Time

❶ Using the information you have read, design a board game for a younger student. Base it on the game of snakes and ladders. On your board, show the situation for black people after the Civil War up to the early twentieth century.

a Use events from the list below. Decide which events made life better (a ladder) for black people and which made life worse (a snake).
- The fourteenth and fifteenth Amendments give black people equal rights
- The Freedmen's Bureau is set up in 1865
- More black people can read and write by 1874
- Jim Crow Laws (1890–1910)
- Garvey's black nationalism is popular (1920s)
- The KKK have over five million members by 1920
- NAACP is set up (1910)
- Harlem becomes a popular centre for black music and dance (1920s)
- Black soldiers are attacked (1946)

b Make snakes and ladders cards that show each event and explain how each would be a step forward or backward.

❷ Do you think that there were more positive or negative changes in this period? Discuss this difficult question in groups or pairs.

❸ Copy and finish these sentences. Look back over the last six pages for ideas.
- *Emancipation means ...*
- *Black people in America were emancipated in ...*
- *After emancipation black people could ...*
- *Segregation means ...*
- *Life was still hard for many black people because ...*

FROM SEGREGATION TO CIVIL RIGHTS: DID THE CIVIL RIGHTS MOVEMENT BRING FREEDOM FOR BLACK PEOPLE?

BLACK PEOPLE IN AMERICA IN THE 1960s

- We have seen that there still wasn't much freedom and equality for black people by the end of the Second World War. In the 1950s black people still faced problems. These included ghetto housing, the worst-paid jobs, segregated schools and transport, and violence from white people.
- Remember that black and white people were supposed to have equal civil rights. This means they should have been treated equally in every way. Did the 1960s bring better civil rights?

What does it mean?

Ghetto
An area of poor, slum housing.

SOURCE 1

Black protestors are beaten by police after a demonstration in Massachusetts in 1964.

SOURCE 2

In 1963 different civil rights groups and churches planned a March on Washington. They wanted equality. Hundreds of thousands of people went on the march, which was peaceful. It was here that Martin Luther King made his famous speech (see page 39).

TAKING ACTION

In the 1950s and 60s black people protested for civil rights in different ways. They held rallies, marches, peaceful sit-ins and **boycotts** of white shops. They also deliberately rode on segregated buses. Look at these different real life stories from the 1960s.

What does it mean?

Boycott
To refuse to support something.

Septima Clark – beating the system. Septima managed to teach black people to pass the literacy tests (see page 31). In the 1950s and 1960s she taught many people to read and write so they passed the test. This gave them a chance to be involved in politics.

Rosa Parkes – bus boycott heroine. Rosa was a 42-year-old seamstress (dressmaker) from Montgomery, Alabama. Rosa was a campaigner for the NAACP.

- **What Rosa did**. After a day at work in December 1955, she sat down on the bus home. But she broke the state law, because she refused to give up her seat to a white person. Rosa was arrested. Because of this she got a lot of publicity.
- **What happened next**. Black leaders in Montgomery organised a mass boycott of the bus system. They wanted to force it to de-segregate (stop segregation). The boycott lasted until 1956 when the Supreme Court said that bus segregation was illegal. The Black leaders had won.
- **Afterwards**. Rosa went on to make speeches at Civil Rights rallies. She also started a school for black children in Detroit.

Little Rock, Arkansas – Police protection just to go to school. The town of Little Rock hit the headlines in September 1957. Nine black children were sent to Little Rock High School, which had been just for white students.

- **What happened**. White mobs surrounded the school, protesting about the black children. The Governor thought they should be sent to an all-black school. But this would be breaking the law.
- **Who got involved**. The President of the USA got involved. Police had to guard the children on their first day. White protesters rioted and President Eisenhower sent in soldiers to make sure the children were let in to school.
- **Afterwards**. The black children were bullied by white children. The nine children became heroes and heroines for black children in the South.

SOURCE 3

There were lots of kids doing what we did. We weren't unusual but we got the attention. We couldn't fight back or we'd be expelled, which might mean the end of integration (mixing black and white). It was very hard for us and our parents. But we had to make integration work.

Elizabeth Eckford was one of the nine black children from Little Rock High School.

Alabama Children's Crusade – a message in numbers. In Alabama a huge campaign was set up to force de-segregation. It included sit-ins and a Children's Crusade.

- **What happened.** In May 1963 a large group of children marched into the white area of town and were arrested for breaking the law. The police jailed over 2000 children. The police also used fire hoses and hurt children when they tried to stop the march.
- **The effects.** The action of the children showed how silly the laws were. Also, the brutal treatment of the police shocked the nation. The Crusade got lots of publicity and public support. But some white people rioted and attacked black people.

FAMOUS CIVIL RIGHTS LEADERS

Martin Luther King and Malcolm X are probably the two most famous civil rights leaders in the USA. Both men were very popular. They worked hard to make life better for black people in America. They had different backgrounds and ideas about the best way to get civil rights. Both men were assassinated for their beliefs.

Activity Time

1 Look at the protests on page 37 and 38. Imagine you are a newspaper journalist. Your editor has asked you to write about one of these protests. What would you write in your story? Use the ideas below to help you.
- Start with a main headline.
- Include two sub-headlines.
- Give a summary of the story.
- Give a short interview with a witness.
- Research for more details and pictures.

Martin Luther King
- Christian Baptist Minister.
- Believed in peaceful protest.
- Wanted black and white people to live together.

Malcolm X
- Spokesperson for a black Muslim group.
- Believed that violence should be fought with more violence.
- Thought that black people would have to live separately.

SOURCE 4

I say to you today, my friends. I have a dream that one day this nation will rise up and live out its beliefs: 'that all men are created equal.'

I have a dream that my four little children will one day live in a nation where they will not be judged by the colour of their skin but by their character.

I have a dream that one day every valley shall be raised, every hill and mountain shall be made low.

All people will be able to join hands and sing: 'Free at last! Free at last! Thank God Almighty, we are free at last!'

Adapted from Martin Luther King's speech at the March on Washington in 1963.

SOURCE 5

If you're interested in freedom, you need some judo, you need some karate. You need all the things that will help you fight for freedom. If we don't resort to the bullet, then we have to take steps now to use the ballot (voting). You don't need a debate. You need some action! So what you and I have to do is get involved. You and I have to be right there breathing down their throats. Every time they look over their shoulders, we want them to see us. It's going to be the ballot or the bullet.

Malcolm X speaking in Audubon, Washington Heights, New York on Easter Sunday, 1964.

SOURCE 6

This is a picture of Martin Luther King (on the left) and Malcolm X (on the right). It was taken in 1964.

Question Time

1 Listen to or re-read the speeches of Martin Luther King and Malcolm X (see page 39) Copy and fill in this chart to compare the two speeches.

	Martin Luther King	Malcolm X
What do they want?		
What sort of words do they use?		
How do they want to bring about change?		

2 Research more about these two men. What can you find out about:
   a their backgrounds
   b how they were educated
   c their actions?

3 Write up your research in a similarities and differences chart.

4 Look at Source 6. Martin Luther King and Malcolm X look as if they agree about things. Use the information about both men on page 38 to explain if they could work as closely as the picture suggests.

5 Why do you think the photograph in Source 6 was taken?
   a To make Malcolm X look good?
   b To get publicity?
   c To bring all black people together?
   Explain your answer to the person next to you.

AMERICA IN THE 1990s – FROM SLAVERY TO EQUALITY?

Martin Luther King and Malcolm X represent the start of progress towards civil rights. Black people are now famous in every area of life including law, politics, films, sport and music. But black people still face many problems, and many are still poor.

Activity Time

Plan a debate about equality between black and white people in the USA today. Half of you will argue that equality exists. The other half will argue that it doesn't. The facts on page 41 will give you some ideas to research. But you will need to find more examples. The list below will help:

   Advertisements   Films   Music industry
   Sports   Politics   Newspaper articles

Each person should have one area to research. Make brief notes of what you can find. For the debate, you will need key speakers, witnesses statements of evidence and a summary statement for each side. Your teacher will give everyone a role to play.

From slavery to equality? What do these facts suggest?

- In 1990 the average income of a black family in USA was less than half that of an average white family.
- In 1992 serious riots started in Los Angeles after four policemen were let off charges of beating up a black man called Rodney King. The attack was caught on video. But the policemen were found not guilty. Most of the jury members on the case were white people.
- In the mainly black slums in the USA's big cities as many as 65 per cent of people are out of work.
- In 1990 fewer than 1 per cent of partners (managers) in law firms were black people.
- Civil rights groups have become less popular.
- The number of black people as mayors increased by four between 1970 and 1990.

Marion Jones, World and Olympic champion in many track and field events.

Will Smith, singer, TV and film star.

Maya Angelou, author of poetry and story books which sell all over the world.

Colin Powell, US Secretary of State. Before this he was Chairman of the Joint Chiefs of Staff, the highest military position in the US Department of Defense.

Unit 16: The franchise – why didn't women get the vote at the same time as men?

Imagine living in a country where only half the people who lived there were allowed to decide how it should be run. This was true of Britain until 1918. Only men could vote in general elections for Members of Parliament, and only men could be Members of Parliament.

WHY DIDN'T WOMEN VOTE?

During the 1800s, many people in Britain believed that women were too weak to be able to think for themselves and take charge of their own lives. At the start of the century, women were not allowed to own any property. They depended on the men in their families – their fathers, husbands and brothers. People thought that:

> **What does it mean?**
>
> **The franchise**
> This is the right to vote in elections. Suffrage means the same thing.

- women should only concern themselves with things to do with their homes and families
- men should concern themselves with things outside the home, like earning money and making laws.

So already we have part of the answer to the question 'Why didn't women get the vote at the same time as men?'

Did everyone believe that women were weaker than men? No! A lot of women and some men did not believe that women were weaker. They believed that women should have a say in the ways the country was run.

THREE CAMPAIGNING WOMEN: WHAT WERE THEY FIGHTING FOR?

We are going to study three women, who each worked very hard to change other women's lives. As you read about the three women, think about what they were fighting for and what methods they used in their struggle.

HARRIET TAYLOR (1807–58)

Harriet was born in 1807. Her father was a London surgeon. When she was 18 years old, she married John Taylor. He was a wholesale chemist. They had three children. Everything seemed fine until, in 1830, she met John Stuart Mill.

Harriet said that John was the first man to treat her as an equal. She decided to leave her husband. Although she lived alone, John visited her at weekends. Many of their friends were so shocked by their behaviour, they wouldn't visit Harriet or John.

Harriet and John wrote many books together. But most of them were published under John's name only. This is because, at that time, it was very difficult for people to accept that women could have serious ideas.

In her writing, Harriet argued that men and women should be treated equally in society and by the law. She wanted laws to protect wives from violent husbands.

SOURCE 1

A portrait of Harriet Taylor.

What does it mean?

The Subjection of Women
A book written by Harriet Taylor and John Stuart Mill. It says that women are under the control of men and that this is wrong.

Equality of women in society and law meant:
- Wives and children should not be thought of as belonging to the husband.
- Married women should be able to keep their own property and their own earnings.
- Women should be able to get a divorce for the same reasons as men.
- Women should be allowed to bring up their children after a divorce.

JOSEPHINE BUTLER (1828–1906)

In 1863, a terrible tragedy hit Josephine and George Butler. Their youngest child, Eva, fell to her death in front of them. To try to get over her grief, Josephine started to do charity work. She decided to help the most disadvantaged women in society – prostitutes.

- Josephine believed that women were forced to become prostitutes because they could not earn a living any other way. She believed that these women were terrified they would have to go into a **workhouse**.
- Josephine thought it was wrong that women were blamed for being prostitutes, yet men were not blamed for using them.
- Two Contagious Diseases Acts tried to stop the spread of sexually transmitted diseases. Under these acts, prostitutes could be forced to have a medical examination. Men using prostitutes did not have to have a medical examination. Josephine argued that this was unfair.
- Josephine campaigned against the unfair treatment of prostitutes by making speeches up and down the country. At the time, it was very unusual for a woman to do this.
- Josephine wrote books asking for better education for women.

Who was she?

The married life of Caroline Norton

Caroline was from a well-off family. She wrote best-selling novels. In 1827 she got married. This meant that the money her father had left her in his will, and all the money she earned from her writing, now belonged to her husband. Her husband was violent and often hit her. Things sometimes got so bad that Caroline had to take their three sons and hide from her husband in the homes of family and friends. Caroline could not divorce her husband because she had to prove he was violent and unfaithful. (Violence alone was not enough.) In 1836, her husband left her. But he took the children with him. She had no right to see them ever again. Caroline campaigned for the law to be changed. In 1839 it was. Mothers were allowed legal custody of their children under the age of seven, as long as the mother had not been unfaithful.

Question Time

1. What reasons might Josephine Butler have given for her campaign to help prostitutes?

2. Think about the life stories of Harriet Taylor and Caroline Norton. What do these stories tell us about how women in nineteenth-century Britain were seen?

EMMELINE PANKHURST (1858–1928)

Emmeline and Richard Pankhurst both supported equal rights for women. Richard (Emmeline's husband) was a lawyer and he and Emmeline were very keen that women should be allowed to vote. She believed that women's living and working conditions would change if they could vote. The vote would give them a voice in Parliament and the power to bring in new laws.

Emmeline and Richard had four children. Two of their daughters, Christabel and Sylvia, also fought for equal rights for women. This included the right to vote.

What was it?

Workhouse
People went to live in workhouses if they were too poor to feed and clothe themselves. The workhouses were run by the local parish. Conditions in workhouses were very bad.

SOURCE 2

In the workhouse, I found pregnant women scrubbing floors and doing all kinds of hard work. They did this right up to the time their babies were born. Many of these women were unmarried and very, very young. When they had their babies they had a choice.

They could either stay in the workhouse and be separated from their babies. Or they could leave with their babies, with nowhere to go and no hope.

An extract from *My Own Story* by Emmeline Pankhurst, published in 1914.

WSPU

In 1903, Emmeline Pankhurst started the Women's Social and Political Union (WSPU). The WSPU organised marches, rallies and petitions to try to persuade people that women should be allowed to vote in general elections. The WSPU had its own magazine, *The Suffragette*. It also tried to get letters and articles published in national newspapers.

By 1905, Emmeline and some other **suffragettes** began to believe that their peaceful methods weren't working. So they turned to violence. They annoyed public speakers at political meetings, set fire to pillar boxes and chained themselves to railings to draw attention to their cause. Many suffragettes were thrown into prison. Some of them went on **hunger strikes**.

The WSPU stopped campaigning when the First World War broke out in 1914. They supported the war effort. But Emmeline made it clear that their campaign for 'votes for women' would carry on when the war ended.

Emmeline died in 1928. In the same year, women got equal voting rights with men.

Who were they?

Suffragettes
Women who wanted votes for women. They used violence in their campaigns.

What does it mean?

Hunger strikes
Sometimes, when people want to draw attention to their cause, they stop eating. This is called a hunger strike. Some suffragettes did this when they were sent to prison for their violent acts.

WHO WAS THE ANGEL IN THE HOUSE?

Harriet, Josephine and Emmeline believed that men and women should be treated equally. Many people disagreed because they thought that men and women had very different parts to play in society.

Coventry Patmore wrote a poem called *The Angel in the House*. In the poem, he describes women as being 'angels' at home, full of love and kindness, always caring for others. He believed this was what women did best. Many people agreed with him. They believed men were stronger than women – physically and mentally.

George Elgar Hicks painted three pictures showing what women should be. One, called *Guide of Childhood*, shows a woman looking after her son. Another, called *Companion of Manhood*, shows a woman comforting her husband. The third, called *Comfort of Old Age*, shows a woman looking after her old father.

The pictures were shown in a London exhibition. Many people went to see them. They bought copies to hang on their walls at home.

SOURCE 3

A painting by George Elgar Hicks. It is called *Woman's Mission: Companion of Manhood* and was exhibited in 1863.

Activity Time

Select information from 'Three campaigning women' (pages 43–6) to make a chart like the one below. You will need at least one side of A4 for your chart.

	Harriet Taylor	Josephine Butler	Emmeline Pankhurst
Dates			
Aims: What was she fighting for?			
Methods: What did she do to achieve her aims?			

❶ Look at the information you have collected on the three women's aims.
a How were these aims the same?
b How were the aims different?

❷ Look at the information you have collected on the three women's methods.
a How were these methods the same?
b How did the methods used by the women change through the period?

❸ All of the women on the following list tried to make a difference to the lives of other women. Choose **one** woman from the list. Then find out as much as you can about her.

- Florence Nightingale
- Mary Seacole
- Mary Kingsley
- Elizabeth Fry
- Mary Shelley
- Annie Besant

Organise your research around these questions.
a What was the woman's background?
b What did she want to achieve?
c How did she try to achieve her aims?
d What opposition did she face?
e What support did she have?
f How successful was she?

Question Time

Look carefully at Source 3 before you answer the questions.

1 The woman in the painting is comforting her husband. He has just found out that someone he knows has died. Describe how the painting tells us these things.

2 Look at how the man and the woman are standing. Then look at the clothes they are wearing. Has the artist painted the woman to look weaker than the man? Explain your answer.

3 Look at the titles of the three paintings mentioned on page 46. What was the artist trying to say about women?

WAS IT THE SAME FOR EVERYONE?

Source 3 shows a middle-class family home. Although most working-class people had the same ideas about the place of women in society, most working-class women worked. They worked because their families needed the money. They worked on farms and as servants in large houses. Later, as more factories were built, they worked as **mill** girls and factory workers. But there were strict rules and customs about the sorts of jobs women could do and the sorts of jobs men should do.

Women were always paid less than men even when their work was the same or very similar. And at home the man was always the head of the house and made all the important decisions. This was the case even though the family needed the woman's wage to survive.

Who were they?

Mill girls
Women and girls who worked in cotton or woollen mills. These were specialised factories where raw cotton or wool were spun into thread and woven into cloth.

The idea of the 'Angel in the House' seemed to apply only to middle-class women. Working-class women often had to work so that their families could be properly fed and clothed.

Activity Time

Copy the diagram below. The circle on the left represents the woman's role in a middle-class family. The circle on the right represents the man's role in a middle-class family.

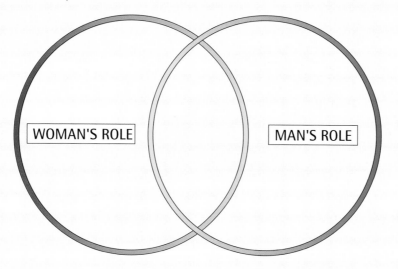

1 Look at the activities below. Which circle do they each belong in? You may want to put some activities in the middle area.

- Earning money
- Owning property
- Sewing
- Drawing
- Playing music
- Joining the army
- Writing books and newspaper articles

- Caring for children
- Managing servants
- Making laws
- Spending money
- Declaring war
- Public speaking

2 Write a paragraph describing what most people in the nineteenth century believed about the role of women. Use your diagram to help you.

3 Write a paragraph describing what most people in the nineteenth century believed about the role of men. Use your diagram to help you. Think also about the activities they were supposed to do.

4 In what ways were the beliefs of these women different?
a Harriet Taylor
b Josephine Butler
c Emmeline Pankhurst

WHY DID SOME PEOPLE HAVE THE VOTE IN 1815 AND NOT OTHERS?

By now, you should have some good ideas on why it took so long for women to get the vote. But in 1815, not many men could vote either. Why was this?

THE POLITICAL SYSTEM IN 1815

Britain was run by Parliament. Parliament was divided into:
- the House of Commons, and
- the House of Lords.

Only men were elected to the House of Commons. Those elected were known as Members of Parliament (MPs). Members of the House of Lords were not elected. When a lord died, his eldest son automatically took over his father's place in the House of Lords. If there was no son, the place passed to the dead lord's nearest male relative.

Constituencies: counties and boroughs

Each MP represented an area of Britain called a constituency. In 1815 these were the counties of England, Scotland and Wales, along with 294 boroughs (towns). These constituencies had been set up in the sixteenth century. The new industrial towns of the Midlands and the north of England were not represented in Parliament.

The franchise: the voters

Only men could vote. But not all men had the vote. It depended on where you lived. You had the right to vote if you owned some land. But the amount of land you needed to own varied from constituency to constituency.

The elections

Voting was not secret. Elections were usually noisy, rowdy affairs. The candidates usually bribed the voters by treating them to vast banquets and plenty of beer. Many elections were controlled by wealthy landowners. They made sure their friends and relatives were elected to the House of Commons.

The candidates: who could become an MP?

Men who wanted to become MPs had to own land or property worth a certain amount of money before they could stand for election. There were two main political parties that MPs could belong to:

- Tories
- Whigs.

What does it mean?

Democratic

The word means 'rule of the people'. In western Europe today, a democracy is a government chosen by the people.

Who were they?

Tories

A political group in Parliament who were mainly land-owning gentry.

Whigs

A political group in Parliament who were mainly supported by bankers, merchants and manufacturers.

Question Time

1. Look at the map. Then answer these questions.
   a What was the population of Sarum?
   b How many MPs did Sarum have?
   c What was the population of Yorkshire?
   d How many MPs did Yorkshire have?

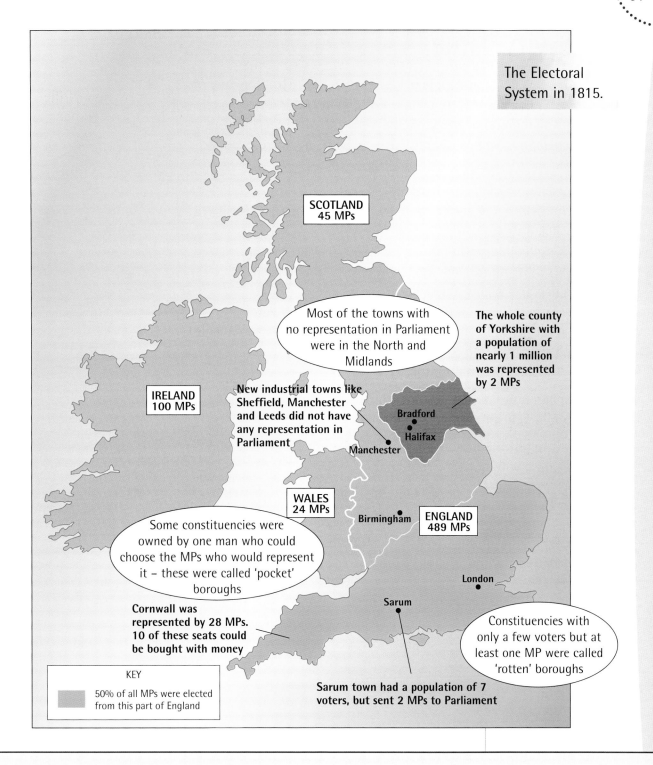

The Electoral System in 1815.

SCOTLAND
45 MPs

IRELAND
100 MPs

Most of the towns with no representation in Parliament were in the North and Midlands

The whole county of Yorkshire with a population of nearly 1 million was represented by 2 MPs

New industrial towns like Sheffield, Manchester and Leeds did not have any representation in Parliament

Bradford
Halifax
Manchester

WALES
24 MPs

Birmingham

ENGLAND
489 MPs

Some constituencies were owned by one man who could choose the MPs who would represent it – these were called 'pocket' boroughs

London

Sarum

Cornwall was represented by 28 MPs. 10 of these seats could be bought with money

Constituencies with only a few voters but at least one MP were called 'rotten' boroughs

KEY

50% of all MPs were elected from this part of England

Sarum town had a population of 7 voters, but sent 2 MPs to Parliament

Do you think that MPs were fairly distributed around the country? Explain your answer.

❷ a Why do you think boroughs like Sarum were called 'rotten'?
b Some boroughs were called 'pocket' boroughs. Find out why they were given this name.

❸ Read the meaning of **democratic**.
a How was the political system in 1815 *not* democratic?
b How was it democratic?

Activity Time

1 Look at the list of people below. The year is 1815. Only one of these people is able to vote. Use the map and the information on pages 50–51 to work out which person it is. *Remember: women did not have the vote. So there are only men in this list.*

- A lawyer living and working in Leeds.
- An undergardener living and working on the small estate of a village vicar.
- A skilled gunsmith renting his house in Manchester.
- A soldier of ordinary rank who has fought against the French and is now unemployed.
- The manager of a woollen factory in Macclesfield.
- A farmer in Devon. He owns a large area of land, woodland and several cottages.
- A shopkeeper in Brighton.

2 Explain how you worked out which person on the list could vote in general elections.

3 How might the person you chose explain to the others why he could vote but they could not?

4 How might a man who could vote explain to his wife why he could vote but she could not?

You may write your answers to Questions 3 and 4 as a conversation, if you would like to.

WHO WAS STRUGGLING FOR POLITICAL CHANGE BETWEEN 1815 AND 1848?

RIOTS AND UNREST

Unemployment and poverty

Immediately after 1815, there was a lot of unemployment and poverty in Britain. The wars against France and America had ended. This meant that:

- thousands of soldiers had come home and couldn't find work
- there was unemployment in the coal and iron industries because weapons were no longer needed.

In 1815 there had been other events that did not help this situation.

- Harvests failed because there was no rain.
- Parliament passed **Corn Laws**. These laws helped the farmers but kept the price of bread high.
- More babies were born so there were many more people to feed.

Working-class people suffered the most from low wages and unemployment. They also had larger families to feed. Food, especially bread, was expensive.

The new industrial towns

- **The working classes**. Thousands of working-class people moved to the new industrial towns to find work in factories and mills. Once there, they found that working and living conditions were terrible. There were no laws to limit the hours they worked or the conditions they worked in. There were no laws, either, to check on how safely houses were built, and no laws about clean water and human waste. Only Parliament could change things. Working-class people could not vote. So they had no one to represent them in Parliament.

What were they?

Corn Laws

These laws were first passed in 1815. They said that cheap foreign corn could not be imported until British corn reached a certain price. This helped farmers. But it kept the price of bread high, which wasn't so good for people who were poor.

Question Time

❶ Why was it important for working-class people to have the vote?

❷ Why did some middle-class people support the demand for more political change?

Explain your answers.

- **The middle class.** Doctors and lawyers, mill owners and developers were all part of the growing middle class. As they became more powerful locally, so they demanded to be heard in Parliament.

Radical ideas

In 1789 the French **Revolution** ended the reign of the king and queen of France. It got rid of the aristocracy and the old way of governing France. Some of the ideas behind the French Revolution spread to Britain. They were used by groups of people who began campaigning for:

- all men in Britain to have the vote
- lower taxes
- more help for poor people.

These ideas were called 'radical' because they would cause big changes in British society if they were introduced.

What does it mean?

Revolution
A huge change. Revolutions can be peaceful or violent. If violence is used, it's usually because people want to see a big change in the system of government.

Who were they?

Radicals
People who wanted big changes in society.

THE FRENCH REVOLUTION – WOULD IT SPREAD TO BRITAIN?

The British government and the land-owning classes looked at the poverty, hunger and unemployment in Britain. They became afraid. The French Revolution had happened partly because of the bad harvests, hunger and poverty. Could the same thing happen in Britain, they wondered?

WHAT HAPPENED ON ST PETER'S FIELD, MANCHESTER IN 1819?

In August 1819, about 60,000 men, women and children gathered in St Peter's Field, Manchester. They had come to listen to speakers talk about the problems that faced them all and about the need for change.

Manchester's magistrates, who were responsible for law and order, were worried about the size of the crowd. They were afraid a riot might start. They sent soldiers in to arrest the speakers. In the panic that followed, 11 people were killed and 400 were seriously injured.

Journalists who were there wrote about what happened. The news spread quickly throughout Britain. People were horrified. British troops had killed their own people at **'Peterloo'**. It was an outrage!

What did the government do? It congratulated the magistrates for their quick action in preventing a worse disaster. The main speaker, Henry Hunt, was sent to prison for two years.

What does it mean?

Peterloo
Radicals nicknamed the killings at St Peter's Field 'Peterloo'. 'Peterloo' sounds a bit like 'Waterloo', where the British had won a battle three years earlier.

SOURCE 1

This drawing of 'Peterloo' was made at the time the meeting happened. The woman on the platform dressed in white is Mary Fildes. She was attacked by soldiers during the meeting. So were some other speakers.

Factfile: Mary Fildes

Mary was a speaker at 'Peterloo'. You can see her in Source 1 on page 55. She was one of the few women to speak in public at this time. What else did she do?

- She was the leader of the 'Manchester Female Reform Group'.

- She believed women should have control over their own lives.

- She believed in birth control.

- She wrote books about birth control. People accused her of spreading pornography because they were not used to discussing the subject.

BUT ...

- She didn't want votes for women.

- She believed that women should support men in their struggle for the vote. This was a view shared by most radicals at the time.

MARCHES, RISINGS AND REVOLUTIONARY PLOTS

Peterloo was not the only time a mass meeting ended in violent clashes with the authorities.

- **Spa Fields**. In 1816, a huge political meeting was held at Spa Fields in London. Henry Hunt, who later spoke at St Peter's Field, was the main speaker. Part of the crowd rioted. They broke into a gun shop and marched to the Tower of London. This march was easily stopped by soldiers and the leaders were arrested.

- **Oliver**. The government used a spy, nicknamed 'Oliver', to investigate suspect groups. He reported on anti-government plots in Yorkshire, Derbyshire and Nottinghamshire. The ringleaders were arrested.

- **The Blanketeers**. Handloom weavers were losing their jobs because the new mechanised power looms were replacing them. Unemployed handloom weavers began a peaceful march from Manchester to London. They wanted to present a **petition** to the government and ask for help. Manchester magistrates used soldiers to stop the march. One man was killed. The marchers were called 'Blanketeers' because of the blankets they carried to keep themselves warm on the march, and also to show that they were weavers.
- **Cato Street conspiracy**. In 1820, government spies found out about a plot to blow up government ministers while they were eating dinner. Five of the plotters were hanged.

WHAT DID THE GOVERNMENT DO?

The government passed a set of laws in 1819 called the Six Acts. These made peaceful political protest impossible. The government refused to consider reform. It was to be another ten years before the House of Commons seriously considered changes to the Parliamentary system.

What does it mean?

Petition

If people want something to happen, or want to stop something from happening, they all sign a piece of paper. This paper then goes to the government.

Question Time

1 Thomas Paine was one of the most important radicals of the eighteenth and nineteenth centuries. Find out what his ideas were. You could use the Internet to help you.

2 Why did the events of 1815–1820 frighten the government?

3 The Six Acts were passed soon after 'Peterloo'. Why do you think they were passed?

WHY DID POLITICIANS START TO THINK ABOUT REFORM?

By 1830, some politicians thought it was time for change. These politicians were in the Whig party. The Whig Prime Minister, Earl Grey, had been interested in reform for some time. But it wasn't until 1830 that the Whigs were powerful enough to try to introduce it in Parliament.

What reforms did Grey want?

Earl Grey did *not* want to give the vote to all men, and he certainly did not want women to have the vote. He wanted just enough **reform** to satisfy the middle class. He thought that then they would stop supporting the radical ideas of the working class. Earl Grey was influenced by the ideas of Edmund Burke.

What were Edmund Burke's ideas?

Edmund Burke said that all living things change gradually. If they don't change to fit their situation, they will die. He said that Parliament was like a living thing. If it didn't change to fit new circumstances, it would eventually die. It might even be destroyed by revolution, which is what happened in France.

How did this influence Earl Grey?

Grey told Parliament that Britain had changed since the eighteenth century. This meant that the political system had to change, too. Grey told them that the most important change was that the middle class had got larger. Middle-class people wanted a say in how Britain was run. He explained that giving the middle class more power would stop them supporting radical ideas like votes for all men.

What does it mean?

Reform

Change or improvement, usually by bringing in laws to make things fairer.

SOURCE 2

A portrait of Edmund Burke.

Activity Time

You are an adviser to Earl Grey. The year is 1830.

1 What was Grey's main aim? Write it out.

2 Read the three pieces of advice set out below. Choose the advice that Grey should take so that he will achieve his main aim.

a No change should be made to the political system. The government should carry on ignoring radicals and their demands.

b Small changes should be made. The vote should be given to the middle class who own property but not to the working class.

c Big changes should be made. The vote should be given to all men. Later on, the government should think about giving votes to women.

Which piece of advice will you give Earl Grey? Explain why you chose this piece of advice.

THE GREAT REFORM BILL IS PASSED

The bill in Parliament

Earl Grey introduced a reform bill in 1831. It passed the first stage by one vote. But it was defeated at the next stage. Grey resigned. A general election was called, and Grey and the Whigs were voted back into power. Grey got the bill through the House of Commons. But it was promptly thrown out by the House of Lords.

Riots

There were riots and demonstrations all over Britain in support of Grey and reform. Newspapers that supported reform appeared with black edges. Muffled bells tolled as a sign of mourning.

Back to Parliament

Grey resigned again and the **Duke of Wellington** (the Tory leader) tried to introduced a more limited reform bill. That was thrown out and Grey was soon back again. Eventually the King had to get involved and the House of Lords finally let the reform bill through. The long struggle in Parliament had taken more than a year.

Who was he?

The Duke of Wellington
He led the British troops to victory over the French at the Battle of Waterloo. Later, he led the Tory party and was bitterly opposed to reform.

SOURCE 3

George Cruikshank, a well-known cartoonist of the time, published this drawing in 1832. The tree represents the old Parliamentary system. Those people in favour of reform are trying to cut down the tree. Those who are against reform are trying to prop it up.

Question Time

1 Do you think George Cruikshank was for or against Parliamentary reform? Use the details in Source 3 to help you explain your ideas.

2 Do you think the cartoon was published before or after the reform bill of 1831 was passed? What are your reasons?

WHAT DID THE GREAT REFORM ACT OF 1832 CHANGE?

Political System before 1832	Political System after 1832
CHANGES TO THE FRANCHISE (the qualification to vote)	
• Who could vote in boroughs varied greatly from place to place	• Who could vote in the boroughs became the same everywhere – householders with property worth a certain amount, which included most of the middle classes
• 13 per cent of the adult male population could vote	• 18 per cent of the adult male population could vote
CHANGES TO THE CONSTITUENCIES (how votes and MPs were distributed)	
• Many towns and cities in the Midlands and north had no MPs	• 65 MPs given to some of these areas
• Many rotten boroughs	• 56 rotten boroughs abolished
	• 30 other rotten boroughs now elected only 1 MP instead of 2
	• 41 new boroughs created
• Nearly 200 pocket boroughs	• 130 pocket boroughs abolished

WHAT DID THE GREAT REFORM ACT NOT CHANGE?

- The people who could vote in county elections did not change. This meant that landowners could still influence elections.
- People still voted in the open, so everyone knew who they had voted for. Voters could still be bribed or forced to vote for the person the landowner wanted to be elected.
- Men still had to be wealthy property owners before they could become MPs.

Activity Time

❶ Read carefully the two sections 'What did the Great Reform Act of 1832 change?' and 'What did the Great Reform Act not change?'. Use the information there to make two lists:
- List A: improvements
- List B: no change.

❷ What, in the Great Reform Act, was there that might cause trouble later?

CHARTISM: A WORKING CLASS-MOVEMENT

Working-class people were disappointed with the Great Reform Act of 1832. So were the radicals. The Act had given the vote to middle-class men but not to working-class men. The poorer people of Britain could not persuade Parliament to help them unless they had the vote.

After 1832 many working-class people and radicals got together. They demanded change to the political system. Their demands were written up in a document called a 'Charter'. People who supported the Charter were called 'Chartists'.

SIX POINT CHARTER

Universal male suffrage

Secret ballot

Annual elections

Payment of MPs

No property qualification for MPs

All constituencies to have equal numbers of voters

Activity Time

1 Work in pairs or small groups. Copy out the six points of the Charter on to a large sheet of paper. Discuss each point in turn. Then, next to each point, write:
a what it means
b how it would make Britain more democratic.

Here's an example for point 4.

a Payment of MPs means paying a salary to Members of Parliament.

b In the 1830s, MPs had to be wealthy. This was because they were not paid a salary. If MPs were paid a salary, working-class people could afford to give up their jobs to become an MP.

WHAT HAPPENED TO THE CHARTISTS?

The Chartists presented three petitions to Parliament. They all asked for the political system to be changed. They were all rejected. After the final petition, taken to Parliament in 1848, the Chartist movement came to an end.

WHY DID CHARTISM FAIL IN 1848?

There are several reasons why the Chartist movement failed in 1848.

1 Chartists were not a united group

- The main division was between Chartists who thought the Charter should be gained by peaceful methods, and Chartists who said that violence was the only way.
- There were different Chartist groups in different parts of the country. These had different leaders who had different ideas about what they wanted and how to set about getting it.

2 The government was well prepared to deal with Chartist riots and rebellion

- The new railways meant that soldiers could be moved quickly to trouble spots.
- The new telegraph system meant that information could be passed quickly around the country.

The Chartism movement was not a success. But it wasn't a complete failure either. More and more working people joined organisations, like **trade unions**, to fight for their rights. By 1928, all but one of the Chartists' demands had been met.

What does it mean?

Trade union

An organisation that looks after workers who have a particular trade (skill). For example, people who work on the railways have a union that looks after them.

SOURCE 4

Poor creatures, their threats of attack are miserable. With half a cartridge, and half a pike, with no money, no discipline, no skilful leaders, they would attack soldiers with leaders, money and discipline, who are well-armed and have 60 rounds of bullets each.

General Napier wrote this about some Nottingham Chartists in 1839. Napier was in charge of law and order.

SOURCE 5

The 1830s and early 1840s were times of great poverty for working-class people. This was also a time when Chartism was very popular with them. In the middle of the 1840s there was less unemployment, hunger and poverty, and Chartism was less popular. A sudden rise in unemployment in 1847 led to an increase in Chartist activity until living conditions improved in the 1850s.

A modern historian writing about why Chartism ended in 1848.

WHY DIDN'T THE CHARTISTS CAMPAIGN FOR VOTES FOR WOMEN?

All Chartists wanted every man in the country to have the vote. Very few of them wanted women to have the vote at the same time. This was because they thought it would be more difficult to persuade Parliament to give the vote to all men and all women. So they concentrated, first, on getting the vote for all men.

Two Chartists who did believe in votes for women

Elizabeth Pease and Anne Knight were two Chartists who did believe in votes for women as well as for men.

- Elizabeth Pease complained that her family and friends called her 'unladylike' because she supported votes for women.
- Anne Knight was angry at the lack of support she had from men and women Chartists. She criticised the Chartists, too, because they did not allow women to have positions of power inside the movement.

SOURCE 6

FELLOW COUNTRYWOMEN! We call on you to join us and help our fathers, husbands and brothers to free themselves. We have been told that the place for a woman is in her home. We have been told that politics should be left to men. We deny this. Is it not true that the interests of our fathers, husbands and brothers ought to be ours? Our husbands are over-worked. Our houses are half-furnished. Our families are ill-fed. And our children are uneducated. The fear of want hangs over our heads. We are powerless because we are poor.

Written in a leaflet called *To the Women Chartists of Newcastle-upon-Tyne* by Anne Knight. It was published in the *Northern Star* newspaper on 9 February 1849. Anne was trying to persuade the Newcastle women Chartists to support the vote for all men and women.

Question Time

1 Read Source 6. Why did Anne Knight think women should have the vote?

2 Anne Knight wrote political and **feminist** slogans. She printed these on to labels and stuck them on to envelopes.
a Do you think this was a good idea?
b Explain your answer.

3 Elizabeth Pease's friends said it was unladylike to campaign for votes for women. How is this backed up by Source 6?

WHY DID MORE PEOPLE GET THE VOTE IN THE SECOND HALF OF THE NINETEENTH CENTURY?

In 1867 the Second Reform Act was passed. As a result of this Act:

- twice as many men as before could vote
- more men in the counties could vote, including some farmers who rented land
- more MPs were given to industrial towns where there were more people
- MPs were taken away from rural areas where there were fewer people.

All of these measures meant that:

- 36 per cent of the male adult population could vote (this was an increase of 18 per cent)
- working-class voters were the largest group of voters in towns and cities.

What does it mean?

Feminist
Someone who fights for the rights of women.

WHY WAS THE 1867 REFORM ACT PASSED?

It is important to know *why* things happened. It is also important to understand why things happened when they did, and not beforehand or afterwards.

There were several reasons the Second Reform Act was passed in 1867 and not before.

- **1846** The Corn Laws were no longer in force. Food prices were no longer being kept artificially high.

- **1850s** Living standards rose. More people had more money and more food than they had in the 1840s. Parliament began to talk about reform.

- **1854** The Crimean War kept the government busy. People were more interested in who would win rather than political reform.

- **1860s** Some European countries began changing their political systems.

- **1864** A group called the 'National Reform Union' was set up. It put pressure on the government to make the political system more democratic. Many members had been Chartists before 1848. Some politicians were worried it would lead to unrest and riots.

- **1866** There were demonstrations for political reform in various parts of the country. In London, there was a riot. Some politicians were afraid of revolution. Others believed that by giving the vote to more men, revolution would be avoided.

SOURCE 1

There are things that women can do better than men. There are things they cannot do as well. In everything that needs physical force, firmness of character and intelligence, men are better. In things that need mildness, softness of character and friendliness, women are best.

An MP debating the Second Reform Act on 20 May 1867.

Question Time

❶ Read the six statements, which help to explain why political reform happened in the 1860s. Put them in order of importance.

❷ In groups of four, compare and discuss the differences in your orders of importance. Draw up a single list you all agree on.

❸ Read Source 1. Does it agree with what you have learned so far about attitudes to women? Explain your answer.

AND MORE REFORM – WHY?

After 1867, more reform was needed. This was mainly because there were still big differences between who could vote in the towns and who could vote in the countryside.

1884: the Third Reform Act was passed by Parliament

- This Act gave the vote to all male householders in the counties and in the boroughs.
- It made the constituencies more equal in that they had more or less the same number of people in them.
- It gave each constituency one MP.

1872: the Secret Ballot Act made the political system fairer

- The Act meant that people could vote in secret.
- Landowners, bosses and the rich did not know how people voted. So they could no longer control elections.

By 1900: 65 per cent of adult men could vote in general elections

- Those who couldn't vote were men who didn't have their own households. This could be because, for example, they were servants in someone else's house.

Date	Percentage of adult men (over 21) allowed to vote
1831	13
1832	18
1867	36
1884	65

Question Time

❶ In the nineteenth century, the working class were the largest group in the population.
Why do you think that a lot of upper-class people did not want working-class men to get the vote?

❷ The demands of the Six Point Charter were:
- Universal male suffrage
- Secret ballot
- Annual (yearly) elections
- Payment of MPs
- No property qualification for MPs (you did not have to own a house to vote)
- All constituencies to have an equal number of voters.

a How many of these demands had been achieved by 1900?
b List the demands that had not been achieved.

WHAT FREEDOMS WERE WOMEN OBTAINING?

Towards the end of the nineteenth century, there were signs that the role of women was changing.

- In 1870 the government set up a system of primary school education for boys and girls. The schools were called elementary schools.
- In 1880 the government made elementary school education compulsory for boys and girls.
- Women were needed as teachers. By 1900, 75 per cent of teachers were women.
- Women began working as secretaries, clerks, telephonists, shop assistants and nurses.

All these women had to give up their jobs when they got married.

WOMEN'S FIRST STEPS TOWARDS EQUALITY WITH MEN

Activity Time

❶ You are going to find out how the law was changed to give more rights to women. Research the laws below so that you can answer the questions.

• **1857** The Marriage and Divorce Act was passed. The Act gave a married woman the right to own property if her husband left her. It also said women could divorce their husbands if they could prove cruelty, incest or sodomy, as well as adultery.
What did men have to prove?
What did this law say about a mother's right to her own child?

• **1870** An act was passed that said women could keep their own money and property acquired after they married.
What was the name of this act?

• **1882** The second Married Women's Property Act was passed.
What did it say about women's ownership of property?

• A law was passed to say that men could no longer force their wives to live with them at home.
When was it passed?

❷ These laws showed that there had been changes in how people thought about women. Look back to pages 46 and 47. Re-read the section called 'Who was the angel in the house?' Now read Sources 1 to 4. For each source, say if it shows any evidence that being an 'angel in the house' had changed.

SOURCE 1

I longed to be of some use in the world. But we were born into a particular social class. No one thought we should do anything but amuse ourselves and wait until a suitable husband came along. 'Better any marriage than none', a foolish old aunt used to say.

Charlotte Despard writing about what it felt like to be a young women in the 1850s.

SOURCE 2

To remain single was thought of as a disgrace. An unmarried woman of thirty years of age was called an 'old maid'. After their parents died, what could they do? Where would they go? The only respectable paid work was as a governess with a low salary.

Louisa Garret Anderson, describing attitudes in the 1860s.

SOURCE 3

A girl is not necessarily a better woman because she knows the heights of all the mountains in Europe. But she is much better fitted for her life's work if she knows how to look after a child, cook simple food and clean a house properly.

Written by a school inspector in 1874.

You could put your answers on to a chart like the one below.

	Evidence to show that being an 'angel in the house' had changed
Source 1	
Source 2	
Source 3	
Source 4	

SOURCE 4

The Queen is most anxious for everyone who can speak or write to do their best to stop this mad, wicked folly of 'women's rights' with all its horrors on which her poor, feeble sex seems determined. They forget every sense of womanly feeling and proper behaviour. Lady Amberley ought to get a good whipping.

Queen Victoria on hearing that Lady Amberley had spoken at a meeting in favour of women's rights.

WHO WAS CAMPAIGNING FOR VOTES FOR WOMEN?

The position of women under the law was changing. But the changes were very slow. One big barrier to change was that, because women couldn't vote, they couldn't put pressure on MPs to support change. However, by the 1870s, there was a strong and growing movement throughout the country to get women the right to vote.

SOURCE 1

A poster drawn in 1908 by Emily Harding Andrews for the Artists Suffrage League.

SOURCE 2

There isn't the smallest doubt that if women had the vote they would be paid higher wages. The girls say, 'They don't dare ask a man to do what they ask us to do.' 'Of course not,' say the male trades unionists. 'You see, men have the vote.'

Written by Isabella Ford in 1901, to explain why it was important for industrial women workers to get the vote.

SOURCE 3

At the debate on women's suffrage, Mrs Maconochie spoke against giving the vote to women. She said there were too many women to make it safe. There were 1,300,000 more women than men in the country.

Reported in the *East Grinstead Observer* on 3 June 1911.

SOURCE 4

SOME REASONS WHY WORKING WOMEN WANT THE VOTE

• Because as long as women cannot vote for Members of Parliament, they are not asked what they want.
• Because laws are made that directly affect women's work and the work of their children.
• Because the way to help women is to give them the means of helping themselves.

From a pamphlet published by the National Union of Women's Suffrage Societies (NUWSS) in 1913.

Question Time

1 Study Sources 1 to 4. Use these sources to work out:
  a things in favour of giving women the vote
  b things against giving women the vote.

Write this information on a chart like the one below. Fill in the columns in note form.

In favour	Against

2 Look at the list of people below.
  a In pairs, choose one person listed.
  • Queen Victoria
  • A governess in a gentleman's home
  • A nurse in one of the London hospitals
  • The owner of a woollen mill in Leeds with a large workforce of men and women
  • A captain in the army
  • A farmer in Norfolk
  b Discuss whether this person would be in favour of women getting the vote or against it.
  c Hold a conversation with another pair. Talk about the views of your chosen person and listen to the views of their person.

WHAT METHODS DID THE CAMPAIGNERS USE?

People who wanted women to get the vote did not agree on the methods that should be used to get it. Some believed that peaceful methods like marches, demonstrations, petitions and letters to the newspapers would win the day. Others thought that direct action was needed – heckling MPs at meetings, law breaking and even violence.

Women and men all over Britain had campaigned for political equality for women since the 1860s. They gave talks, and wrote pamphlets and newspaper articles. They also collected signatures for petitions that were presented to Parliament.

There were a lot of different groups all over the country, all working for women's suffrage.

Suffragists

In 1897 Millicent Fawcett became leader of the National Union of Women's Suffrage Societies (NUWSS), which united many campaigning groups. Their methods were peaceful. They produced a journal called *The Common Cause*, made speeches and presented petitions to Parliament. By 1914, they were the largest suffrage organisation.

Suffragettes

In 1903 Emmeline Pankhurst set up the Women's Social and Political Union (WSPU). The Union's motto was 'Deeds, not words'. They thought the peaceful methods of the suffragists were getting nowhere. In 1905 the suffragettes decided to take **militant** action, sometimes breaking the law. This would give publicity to their cause and get Parliament to agree to give women the vote.

SOURCE 5

The Suffragette is militant. She tries to force Cabinet Ministers and MPs to give her interviews. Large numbers of police have to be called out to protect them from this interference. Suffragettes prefer to go to prison than the quiet comfort of their own fireside.

The Suffragist is a much quieter lady. She does not believe in the tactics of the war-like Suffragette. She is content to press peacefully for the right to vote.

From the *South London Press,* March 1908.

SOURCE 6

This drawing was on the front cover of the NUWSS pamphlet published in 1914.

The Liberals in power

In 1906 the Liberal party won the general election. Many people hoped that this new government would give women the vote. When this did not happen, the suffragettes became more militant. They smashed windows, set fire to pillar boxes and dyed the water in reservoirs purple. Some chained themselves to railings.

Suffragettes who broke the law were arrested. They were put on trial and some went to prison. Once in prison, suffragettes claimed to be political prisoners. They said they should be treated differently from other prisoners. When the government refused to do this, some suffragettes went on hunger strike.

Hunger strikes and force-feeding

The government did not want a single suffragette to die in prison. They were afraid that this would increase public support for the cause of votes for women. So, from 1909, the suffragettes were force-fed. They had tubes pushed down their throats and into their stomachs. Then liquid food was poured in. This was painful and humiliating. But the women put up with it because of the publicity it gave their campaign.

Question Time

1 Look at Source 6. Read the text at the bottom of the poster.
 a What do the names on the branches represent?
 b What do the numbers in the leaves represent?
 c What does the image say about the NUWSS?

2 What message was the WSPU sending out with their motto 'Deeds, not words'?

3 Force-feeding of hunger strikers won support for the suffragettes. Why do you think this was the case?

Cat and Mouse Act, 1913

This Act said that when hunger-striking suffragettes became dangerously weak, they could be released from prison. Once they had recovered their strength and health, they could be re-arrested. This Act was nick-named the 'Cat and Mouse Act'.

Propaganda

Suffragettes and suffragists both used propaganda as part of their tactics. Source 7 is an example of WSPU **propaganda**.

What does it mean?

Propaganda

Information that gives a particular opinion or view on something. This information could be true or false. It is used to gain support for a cause.

SOURCE 7

A 1910 front cover of the WSPU journal, *Votes for Women*.

Question Time

1 Look at Source 7. What do you think it tells us about the Liberal government?

2 Source 7 was drawn by 'A. Patriot'. Why do you think the artist chose this name?

3 Why do you think the government was quick to pass the Cat and Mouse Act in 1913?

4 Why do you think the Act of 1913 was known as the 'Cat and Mouse Act'?

Activity Time

Copy the grid below into your file.
a Think about the methods used by the suffragettes.
b Think about the methods used by the suffragists.
Fill in the grid with as many examples as you can.

	Methods of the NUWSS	Methods of the WSPU
1897		
1903		
1906		
1909		
1913		

WHY DID WOMEN GAIN THE VOTE IN 1918 AND NOT BEFORE?

By the summer of 1914, the government was prepared to discuss votes for women. But in September, the First World War broke out and everything else was put aside. The suffragettes were let out of prison. The WSPU stopped their militant activities and threw their energies into war work.

Women and the war

Women helped to win the war. They were needed to do the work that had been done by the men who were away fighting. Women worked as railway guards, window cleaners and farm workers. They worked in munitions factories making guns, bullets and shells. Inside their homes, women's work was vital. Feeding their families and caring for the children was difficult with the men away and with wartime shortages. But the women were bringing up the next generation, and this was important.

Vera Brittain

Vera Brittain was from a middle-class family. During the war, she worked as a nurse. She travelled alone and mixed with all sorts of different people. Her father asked her to come home. But she no longer wanted the narrow, boring life she had led before the war.

SOURCE 1

Nothing can stop me doing what I am doing now. I should never respect myself again if I let a few hardships make me give up the finest work a girl can do. I do not agree that my place is at home doing nothing. Anyone who is young and capable should go where they are needed and do the work that has to be done.

From *Testament of Youth,* by Vera Brittain, written in 1933 recalling the war years.

SOURCE 2

During the war, men and women mixed together in ways that would have been impossible before the war. Many girls used language that would have shocked their mothers. They started using cosmetics. They smoked cigarettes and they went drinking in public houses. By the end of the war, 30 per cent more babies had been born to single mothers than in the years before 1914.

Louise Black remembers the war years.

SOURCE 3

Working in the munitions industry was dangerous. Women's skin turned yellow and the toxic poisoning could cause death. There was always the risk of explosions. But women liked munitions work. This was because the pay was higher, other jobs were worse and the strong feeling that working in munitions was the right thing to do in wartime.

From a book by Sheila Robotham, written in 1999, describing the dangers for women working in the munitions industry.

SOURCE 4

A poster urging women to enrol as munitions workers.

Question Time

❶ Look at Source 4. How is it trying to persuade women to become munitions workers?

❷ Now read Source 3. Munitions work was clearly dangerous. Why do you think the poster (Source 4) didn't mention this?'

❸ a From the text and Sources 1 to 3, find different ways in which women helped to win the war.
b Show your findings on a poster titled 'How women helped to win the war!'

❹ Jane Cox, a munitions worker, said: 'The war taught women to stand on their own feet. It was the turning point for women.' Find evidence from pages 76 and 77 that supports what Jane says.

ON HER THEIR LIVES DEPEND

WOMEN MUNITION WORKERS

Enrol at once

VOTES FOR WOMEN!

The part women played in the war convinced many people that the time had come to give them the vote. In February 1918 an Act of Parliament came into force that gave the vote to:

- all men over the age of 21
- women over the age of 30 who were householders
- women over the age of 30 who were wives of householders
- women over the age of 30 who paid rent of more than £5 a year
- women over the age of 30 who were graduates.

Gradually, people accepted that giving the vote to women hadn't resulted in anything disastrous. In 1928, women were given the vote on the same terms as men. Now all women over the age of 21 could vote.

SOURCE 5

I have seen great days, but this was the greatest. I never believed that equal votes would come in my lifetime. But when an impossible dream comes true, we must go on to another. The true unity of men and women is one such dream.

Charlotte Despard said this in 1919, when she was 83.

SOURCE 6

A 1928 cartoon from the magazine *Punch*.

Question Time

1 The Act of 1918 changed the voting system for men, and introduced votes for women for the first time. But the voting system for men and women was still not equal.
a Which men and which women could vote in the general elections?
b Why do you think there were these differences?

2 How did the First World War help to change attitudes towards women?

WHY DIDN'T WOMEN GET THE VOTE AT THE SAME TIME AS MEN?

Activity Time

You are going to use what you have learned to answer the big question: Why didn't women get the vote at the same time as men?

1 Working in groups, you are going to present your findings as a giant poster in four sections.
• Section 1 will show nineteenth-century beliefs about who should vote.
• Section 2 will show nineteenth-century beliefs about women.
• Section 3 will show when, why and how ideas about voting changed.
• Section 4 will show when, why and how ideas about women changed.

a Decide which people are going to work on each section.
b Look again at pages 65 to 78. Make notes to help you decide what should go in each section.
c Design and draw the sections, making them as informative as possible.

Unit 17: Divided Ireland – why has it been so hard to achieve peace in Ireland?

Today, the island of Ireland is divided in two:

- Northern Ireland, part of the United Kingdom (UK)
- the Republic of Ireland, an independent country.

Once, the whole of Ireland had been an independent country. Gradually, and mainly by force, it became part of the United Kingdom. The division into north and south happened in 1922. This was the time of the 'Troubles' – a time of hatred, violence and death. For the rest of the twentieth century, Ireland was a troubled island.

There were deep divisions among the Irish people.

- **Religion**. Protestants and Catholics lived in different parts of the same towns.
- **Politics**. Most Protestants were Unionists who wanted Northern Ireland to stay part of the UK. Most Catholics were Nationalists who wanted Northern Ireland to become part of the Republic of Ireland.
- **History**. Catholics and Protestants stuck strongly to their own histories and traditions.

This map shows how Ireland was divided in 1922.

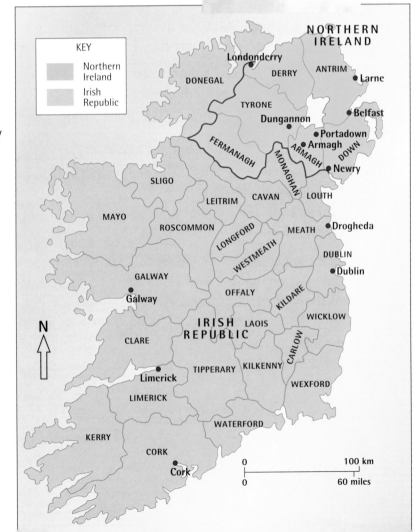

KEY

Northern Ireland

Irish Republic

N

In the 1970s and 80s, Catholics and Protestants expressed their feelings by painting huge designs on the walls of their houses.

SOURCE 1

Wall paintings in Northern Ireland. They were done by Protestants (right) and Catholics (below).

Who was he?

Cuchulainn

Irish legends tell stories about Cuchulainn, who was the son of a Celtic god called Lugh. Cuchulainn was strong and brave. His bravery was so great that he defended the whole of Ireland from attack by evil forces. These evil forces were attacking from inside and outside of Ireland.

Question Time

❶ Look carefully at the two wall paintings in Source 1.

   a Which was painted by the Unionists?
   b Which was painted by the Nationalists?
   c What historical clues have you picked up to help you with your decision?

❷ Read the story of the Irish hero Cuchulainn. This character appeared on both Nationalist and Unionist wall paintings. How could he be a hero to both sides?

WHY IS THE PAST SO IMPORTANT TO SOME PEOPLE IN IRELAND?

We can all look at events in different ways. Football supporters will see a goal as a triumph or a disaster, depending on which side they support. A masked, armed person can be seen as a terrorist or a freedom fighter. It all depends on your point of view. It was like this in Northern Ireland.

WHAT WERE THE FLASH POINTS IN SEVENTEENTH CENTURY IRELAND?

The Plantation of Ulster, 1607

James I was king of Protestant England. In Catholic Ireland, people often rebelled against English rule. James wanted to stop this. He and his advisers worked out a cunning plan. They would send Protestants to live in Ireland.

- First, the English government seized land in Ireland and sacked the Catholic landlords.
- Then they 'planted' English Protestant landlords in their place.

These new Protestant landlords arranged for more Protestants from Scotland and England to settle down in Ireland and farm. But the land they were farming was land that had been seized from Irish Catholics. The Irish Catholics were angry at this **Ulster** 'Plantation' and vowed to take revenge.

The massacre at Portadown, 1641

Catholics in Ireland were afraid that the Protestant English Parliament would pass anti-Catholic laws. In 1641, Catholics in Portadown rebelled and massacred around 3000 Protestant settlers.

What is it?

Ulster
The most northerly of the four original ancient provinces of Ireland, made up of nine counties.

Charles I wanted to send an army to Ireland to fight the rebels. He asked Parliament for money to pay for it. But Parliament suspected that Charles was a secret Catholic. They were afraid he would use the army against his enemies in England. An MP, John Pym, said that Parliament, and not the King, should control any army that was sent to Ireland.

Cromwell in Ireland

Charles I was executed in 1649 and Parliament ruled England. Almost immediately, Irish Catholics began a rebellion against Parliamentary rule. Oliver Cromwell and Parliament were determined to teach the Irish a lesson.

The massacre at Drogheda, 1649

When Cromwell arrived in Ireland, he began killing Catholics. The worst massacre happened in Drogheda, north of Dublin. Cromwell's 12,000-strong army and siege weapons blasted their way into the town. The next day, in cold blood, they massacred 3500 men, women and children.

SOURCE 1

The picture of Catholics murdering Protestant settlers was drawn in 1641. It was probably a propaganda picture.

Driuinge Men Women & children by hund: reds vpon Briges & cafting them into Riuers, who drowned not were killed with poles & shot with muskets.

Question Time

❶ Make a chart like the one here. Use the information on pages 82 and 83 to fill in your chart.

	Portadown	Drogheda
When did it happen?		
Who was killed?		
Who did the killing?		
Why?		

FAST FORWARD

On page 86, we will look at Ireland in the twentieth century. But quite a lot happened between 1649 and 1900, as this timeline shows.

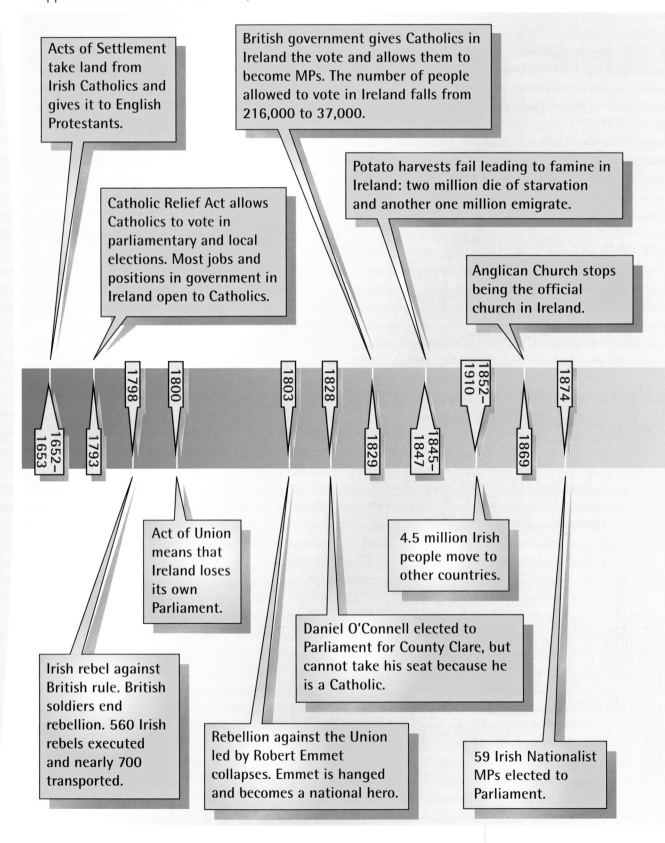

Acts of Settlement take land from Irish Catholics and gives it to English Protestants.

British government gives Catholics in Ireland the vote and allows them to become MPs. The number of people allowed to vote in Ireland falls from 216,000 to 37,000.

Catholic Relief Act allows Catholics to vote in parliamentary and local elections. Most jobs and positions in government in Ireland open to Catholics.

Potato harvests fail leading to famine in Ireland: two million die of starvation and another one million emigrate.

Anglican Church stops being the official church in Ireland.

1652–1653

1793

1798

1800

1803

1828

1829

1845–1847

1852–1910

1869

1874

Act of Union means that Ireland loses its own Parliament.

4.5 million Irish people move to other countries.

Daniel O'Connell elected to Parliament for County Clare, but cannot take his seat because he is a Catholic.

Irish rebel against British rule. British soldiers end rebellion. 560 Irish rebels executed and nearly 700 transported.

Rebellion against the Union led by Robert Emmet collapses. Emmet is hanged and becomes a national hero.

59 Irish Nationalist MPs elected to Parliament.

Parnell does a deal with the British government: he agrees to support them in return for more protection for Irish tenants.

General Elections end with Irish Nationalist MPs holding balance of power.

Charles Stewart Parnell elected to Parliament. He is the leader of the Land League Campaign, fighting for fairer rents. He is also the leader of the campaign to promote the idea that Ireland should rule itself. This idea was called 'Home Rule'.

Chief Secretary for Ireland and his deputy are murdered in Phoenix Park, Dublin.

Third Home Rule Bill introduced.

Third Reform Act increases Irish voters by four times.

First Home Rule Bill fails in the House of Commons.

Timeline: 1875 · 1879–1882 · 1881 · 1882 · 1884 · 1885 · 1886 · 1893 · 1903 · 1910 · 1912

Irish Land Act gives some protection to tenants.

Nationalist MPs from Ireland hold the balance between the parties in the House of Commons. The government need their support.

British government helps Irish tenants buy their land.

Agricultural depression in Ireland. 'Land War' breaks out in the form of a massive protest because tenant farmers were being turned off their farms.

Prime Minister Gladstone announces that he supports Home Rule. This would end the Act of Union and set up an independent Parliament for the whole of Ireland in Dublin.

Second Home Rule Bill gets through Commons, but is defeated in the Lords.

WHY WAS IRELAND PARTITIONED?

'Partition' means 'split in two'. That's just what happened to Ireland in 1922. As you read through the events that led to Partition, remember the following things. Irish Nationalists were Republicans, usually Catholic, who wanted a free and independent Ireland. Irish Unionists were usually Protestants. They wanted to keep the Union with Britain.

WHAT WERE THE EVENTS LEADING UP TO THE DECISION TO PARTITION IRELAND?

- In August 1914 the First World War broke out.
- Irish Catholics and Irish Protestants joined the British army to fight Germany in the First World War.
- Two extreme Irish Nationalist groups, Sinn Fein and the Irish Republican Brotherhood, formed an armed group, the Irish Volunteers. This group rebelled against the British.
- On Easter Monday 1916 the Irish Volunteers took control of Dublin after five days of fighting. Many soldiers, Irish volunteers and ordinary people were killed.
- In the 1918 General Election, Sinn Fein won 73 of the 105 Irish seats. But the Sinn Fein MPs refused to come to Parliament in London. They set up their own Parliament, the Dail Eireann, in Dublin.
- The Irish Volunteers became the Irish Republican Army (IRA).
- From 1919 to 1922 there was war in Ireland between the IRA and the 'Black and Tans', who were ex-soldiers recruited into the Irish police. Hundreds of Irish people were killed.
- In December 1921, an Anglo-Irish treaty divided Ireland between British Ulster in the north and the Irish Free State in the south.

Question Time

❶ Read through the events on the left carefully. For each event, work out:
a what the Unionist reaction would have been
b what the Nationalist reaction would have been.

Remember, the Unionists wanted to stay united with Britain. The Nationalists wanted independence, and were now calling themselves Republicans.

❷ In August 1916, Roger Casement was hanged in London as a traitor. Irish Republicans said he was a hero. See if you can find out why.

WHY DID DAVID LLOYD GEORGE DECIDE THAT PARTITION WAS THE ONLY SOLUTION?

The Dail Eireann

After the General Election of 1918, Sinn Fein refused to take their seats in Parliament in London. Instead, they set up an Irish Parliament in Dublin. But 26 Unionists were elected to Parliament in London at the same time, and they did take up their seats. So when Irish matters were discussed in the London Parliament, only the views of the Protestant Irish Unionists were heard.

Lloyd George suggests two parliaments

Lloyd George, the British Prime Minister, had a solution to the problem. He suggested that there should be two Parliaments in Ireland:

- one in Dublin
- one in Belfast.

Eventually they might join up and become a united Ireland. But both the Unionists and Nationalists were unhappy with parts of what Lloyd George was proposing. So the idea never got started.

The IRA

Meanwhile, the IRA turned to violence. By 1920, there was full-scale war in Ireland between the IRA and the British. The British troops were **demobbed** soldiers known as the Black and Tans. They were hardened by fighting in the First World War. The war was terrible, with violence committed by both sides. The Black and Tans specialised in burning down whole towns and villages. This made more and more people join the IRA.

What does it mean?

Demobbed
This word is short for 'demobilised', meaning the discharge of an individual serviceman or woman from the army, navy or air force.

SOURCE 1

This row of houses was burnt down by the Black and Tans in 1921.

SOURCE 2

These railway wagons were burnt by the Dublin brigade of the IRA when they attacked in 1920.

SOURCE 3

A loyal and Protestant Ulster is important to the British Empire. It would be a marvellous base for the British navy and army to work from if there was serious trouble in Ireland or elsewhere.

A Protestant man living in Ulster explains why he wants to keep Ulster independent from Dublin. He wrote this in a leaflet in April 1920.

SOURCE 4

We will continue to deny the right of any foreign country to exercise power in Ireland. We shall refuse to allow our country to be carved up and partitioned by this foreign country.

A Sinn Fein leader, Eamon De Valera, explains why he doesn't want Partition, July 1923.

Question Time

1 Look at the map below. Why do you think the politicians drew the partition line where they did?

2 Working in groups, write four headings on a large sheet of paper.
- Heading 1: Why Lloyd George had to do something
- Heading 2: Why Lloyd George couldn't ignore the Nationalists' claim to independence
- Heading 3: Why Lloyd George couldn't ignore the Unionists' claim to union with Britain
- Heading 4: Our views – did Lloyd George have any choice?

Sort out the information and sources on pages 87 and 88 so that it fits under these headings. Compare what your group has done with other groups in your class.

This map shows the number of Catholics and Protestants in the counties and large towns of Ulster in 1926. A population survey was made in this year. It is the closest survey to 1922, the year of Partition.

KEY
- Boundary of Ulster
- Boundary of Northern Ireland
- County boundary
- County town
- Protestants
- Catholics
- Other religion

Percentage of population Total NORTHERN IRELAND

Percentage of population Total ULSTER

HOW WAS THE ANGLO-IRISH TREATY DECIDED?

People grew weary and disgusted by the violence and atrocities in Ireland. In July 1921, there was a truce and Eamon De Valera, President of the Dail Eireann, met British Prime Minister David Lloyd George.

- Lloyd George wanted the whole of Ireland to have Home Rule (government based in Ireland, but under the control of Britain).
- De Valera wanted a completely independent Ireland.

A treaty was finally signed on 6 December 1921, but only after the British threatened to start the war again. The Treaty said that Ireland would become a Free State (later called Eire). Six counties in Ulster (later called Northern Ireland) would stay part of the UK.

The Irish Dial Eireann didn't like this arrangement. But they were forced to agree. They accepted the Treaty by 64 votes to 57.

DID ULSTER AND THE FREE STATE DEVELOP DIFFERENTLY AFTER 1922?

Yes, they did. Both parts of Ireland faced enormous political, economic and social problems. The two governments tackled them in different ways.

WHAT HAPPENED IN THE IRISH FREE STATE?

- An economic slump in the 1920s meant that the government didn't have enough money to improve conditions for people.
- Thousands of Irish people moved overseas.
- The country's name was changed to Eire.
- Gaelic became the official language.
- The Catholic Church became the official church. This meant that contraception and divorce were forbidden.
- Eire was neutral in the Second World War.

WHAT HAPPENED IN ULSTER?

- During the economic slump, Ulster stayed reasonably prosperous. This was because it was united with Britain.
- Troops from Ulster fought with troops from the rest of Britain during the Second World War.
- The British welfare state helped everyone in Ulster. They had pensions, free education and a free national health service.
- Contraception and abortion became legal in Northern Ireland at the same time as in the rest of Britain.
- The assembly (parliament) of Northern Ireland met in Stormont Castle. It was dominated by Protestants.
- Protestants dominated the police force, which was called the Royal Ulster Constabulary (RUC).
- There was **discrimination against Catholics**. This means that Catholics were not treated the same as Protestants.

WHY WERE THERE VIOLENT PROTESTS IN NORTHERN IRELAND IN 1968–9?

Divisions between Catholics and Protestants became deeper and deeper. Northern Ireland gradually became a place of suspicion, mistrust and fear.

Activity Time

Work in pairs. Use a large outline map of Ireland to show how the new Ulster and the Irish Free State developed differently.

- Use the information on pages 90 and 91 to help you.
- You can use pictograms, information boxes – anything you think will make your map more informative and lively.

What does it mean?

Discrimination against Catholics

Here are some examples of discrimination against Catholics.

- In County Fermanagh, there were 75 school bus drivers. But only 7 of these were Catholic.
- The Belfast shipyard employed 10,000 workers. But only 400 were Catholics.
- Fermanagh County Council built 1589 council houses between 1945 and 1969. But only 568 went to Catholics.
- In Londonderry, none of the heads of the City Council departments were Catholic. They were all Protestant.

CIVIL RIGHTS FOR ALL

People who live in democratic societies believe there are certain freedoms they should have. These include free speech, the right to vote, freedom of religion and the right to be free from discrimination. These things are called civil rights.

In 1967, Catholics in Northern Ireland set up the Northern Ireland Civil Rights Association (NICRA). They wanted these things:

- Equal voting rights in council elections for Catholics and Protestants.
- An end to local councils that were dominated by Protestants.
- An end to discrimination against Catholics by local councils.
- A fair number of council houses for both Catholics and Protestants.
- The end of the Special Powers Act, which gave the RUC more power in an emergency.

Many Protestants felt threatened by the civil rights movement. They could not believe that the Catholic demands were genuinely peaceful. They knew that many Catholics wanted Northern Ireland to be part of the southern Republic of Ireland. They knew that many Catholics supported the IRA. They were afraid.

LONDONDERRY, 5 OCTOBER 1968

Civil rights supporters arranged a march through the Protestant area of Londonderry on 5 October 1968. The Northern Irish government, made up mainly of Protestants, banned the march. The civil rights supporters took no notice of the ban. They started marching. Read Source 1 to find out what happened next.

SOURCE 1

Our route was blocked by a line of police and tenders drawn up across the road about 300 yards from the starting point. We marched into it but failed to force a way through. Gerry Fitt's head was bloodied by the first baton blow of the day. We noticed that another police cordon had moved in from the rear and cut us off. There were no exits from Duke Street in the stretch between the two cordons which moved simultaneously on the crowd. Ordinary people were clubbed to the ground. They were fleeing down the street from the front cordon and up the street from the rear cordon, crashing into one another, stumbling over one another, huddling in doorways, some screaming. A water cannon – the first we had ever seen – appeared. About 100 people had to go to hospital for treatment.

Eamon McCann records his experiences in his book *War and an Irish Town*.

SOURCE 2

Police begin a baton charge in Duke Street, Londonderry, on 5 October 1968.

Question Time

❶ Which gives you a better idea of what happened in Duke Street, Londonderry, on 5 October 1968?
a Source 1? or
b Source 2?
Explain your answer.

❷ Which source is more reliable?
a Source 1? or
b Source 2?
Explain your answer.

❸ Now read Source 3, which gives a different side to the story.
a How does Source 3 disagree with Source 1?
b Why do you think there is a disagreement?

SOURCE 3

Street fighting broke out again in Londonderry tonight (Sunday) and 20 more people were taken to hospital bringing the total injured since yesterday afternoon (Saturday) to 96.

About 800 people surged up a street leading to one of the city gates. But they were forced back by baton charges by police in steel helmets. The crowds regrouped and battles broke out.

A petrol bomb was thrown at a passing police vehicle. The bomb missed the vehicle, but it burned out the street. Water cannons were brought in to put out other fires.

The police asked the marchers to go home. But the marchers ignored them. They broke the placards they were carrying and threw the bits at the police.

Part of a report in *The Times* newspaper, 7 October 1968.

ONE STEP FORWARD?

The Prime Minister of Northern Ireland in 1968 was Terence O'Neill. He tried to introduce the sort of reforms the civil rights movement wanted.

- Local councils were not allowed to take account of religion when they allocated council houses to people.
- An **Ombudsman** was appointed to listen to complaints from Catholics and Protestants, and make decisions.
- Part of the Special Powers Act, which gave the RUC such power, was to be withdrawn as soon as it was safe to do so.
- All local government was to be reformed by 1971.

Catholics were encouraged by these reforms, although Protestants were angry and afraid.

THE BATTLE OF BURNTOLLET BRIDGE, 4 JANUARY 1969

Londonderry people formed the Derry Citizens' Action Committee. They vowed they would work for full civil rights. Londonderry became the centre of discontent and demands. Students organised a three-day march from Belfast to Londonderry. Meanwhile, on 3 January, a Protestant minister called Ian Paisley held a meeting in Londonderry. He urged Protestants to defend their faith against the 'evils' of Catholicism. On 4 January the student marchers, many of whom were Catholic, arrived at a little place called Burntollet. There, they had to cross a narrow bridge. The Protestants were waiting for them. Source 4 tells us what happened next.

What does it mean?

Ombudsman
An official person who looks into complaints.

SOURCE 4

When we came to Burntollet Bridge a curtain of bricks, boulders and bottles brought the march to a halt. Hordes of screaming people wielded planks of wood, bottles, iron bars and cudgels studded with nails. They waded into the march, beating the hell out of the people. What had been a march became a shambles. The attackers were beating marchers into the ditches, and across the ditches into the river. I saw a young fellow getting a thrashing from four or five supporters of Ian Paisley. A policeman looked on.

This was written by Bernadette Devlin in her book *The Price of My Soul*. She took part in the march when she was a student. The book was published in 1969, the same year she was elected as an MP to the British Parliament.

The violence continued throughout the spring and summer of 1969.

SOURCE 5

The Battle of the Bogside, August 1969. Police fought with Catholics for control of part of Londonderry called the Bogside. The police were forced to withdraw.

Northern Ireland was moving towards civil war. The British government decided it could no longer trust the RUC to keep order fairly between Catholics and Protestants. The Northern Ireland government asked Britain for help. On 14 August 1969, British troops were sent to the streets of Belfast and Londonderry to keep law and order.

SOURCE 6

The Downing Street Declaration

1 Northern Ireland will stay part of the United Kingdom until the people of Northern Ireland decide that they want this arrangement to stop.

2 The UK government has to protect the people of Northern Ireland when law and order breaks down. The Northern Ireland government has asked for British troops to be sent to Belfast and Londonderry to help restore law and order. The UK government has agreed to this. The troops will go home when law and order has been restored.

3 The UK government welcomes the Northern Ireland government's determination to treat Catholics and Protestants equally.

This is how the British Prime Minister announced that British troops were being sent to Northern Ireland to help restore law and order.

Question Time

1 Not many Protestants joined the civil rights movement in Ulster. Why do you think this was?

2 'Bernadette Devlin took part in the civil rights march and so her account of what happened at Burntollet Bridge cannot be trusted.'
Explain whether or not you agree with this statement.

3 Read Source 6.
a How would the Catholics be encouraged by what was said?
b How would the Catholics be worried by what was said?
c How would the Protestants be encouraged by what was said?
d How would the Protestants be worried by what was said?

WERE HUMAN RIGHTS ABUSED IN NORTHERN IRELAND?

In 1948, the United Nations agreed to publish a Declaration of Human Rights. It was to be followed by all member nations.

SOURCE 7

Everyone is born free and should be treated equally. Everyone has the following rights.

1. *To live in freedom and safety.*

2. *Not to be a slave.*

3. *Not to be tortured.*

4. *To be treated equally by the law.*

5. *Not to be put in prison without a public trial.*

6. *To be considered innocent until proved guilty.*

7. *To be defended if accused.*

8. *To ask for protection if threatened.*

9. *To travel inside their country.*

10. *To travel out of their country and come back.*

11. *To have whatever religion they choose, or none.*

12. *To think what they like and to discuss their ideas.*

13. *To organise peaceful meetings.*

14. *To take part in their country's political affairs.*

A simplified version of part of the United Nation's Declaration of Human Rights.

A British soldier patrolling the streets of Londonderry in 1970.

Question Time

1 Re-read Source 7 and pages 91 to 98. Make a list of the Human Rights in Source 7. Beside each Right, write a sentence about how it was being broken in Northern Ireland.

2 Look at Source 8.
a Write a caption for this picture that a Protestant Unionist might have written.
b Now write a caption that a Catholic Nationalist might have written.

3 Look back to the captions you wrote for Question 2. Do you think that Catholics and Protestants in Northern Ireland can ever live together peacefully? Explain your answer.

WHY HAS IT BEEN SO HARD TO ACHIEVE PEACE IN IRELAND?

KEY EVENTS 1969–98

1971 Internment (imprisonment of suspected terrorists) introduced to try to reduce terrorist activity.

1972 Increased terrorist activity leads the British Government to suspend the Northern Ireland Parliament and run Northern Ireland directly from London. Violence increases.

1973 The British Government holds a vote in Northern Ireland over whether the people living there want to be part of the Irish Republic. The majority vote 'No'.

1974 15-member power sharing organisation, made up of Protestants and Catholics, is formed in Northern Ireland. Protestant extremists organise a general strike in protest. Power-sharing collapses.

1982 Elections for a Northern Ireland Assembly take place.

1985 British Government invites the government of the Irish Republic to advise them on what should happen in Northern Ireland's affairs. This is opposed by many Protestants.

1986 Northern Ireland Assembly is abolished. Direct rule continues.

1993 Downing Street Declaration about the future of Northern Ireland is signed by British and Irish Prime Ministers.

1994 IRA ceasefire; British Government holds talks with the IRA.

1996 IRA ends ceasefire by exploding a massive bomb in the heart of London's dockland.

1998 Talks between Catholics and Protestants and the British Government result in the Good Friday Agreement.

Referendums held in Northern Ireland and the Irish Republic approve the Good Friday Agreement.

Omagh bomb blast kills 29 people.

1999 Peace process stumbles over the problem of decommissioning (Protestants and Catholics giving up their weapons).

Behind the violence and the hatred, there was a quiet desire for peace among many of the people of Northern Ireland. There were many peace moves as a result of the following things.

- The actions of governments in Britain, the Republic of Ireland and the USA.
- The actions of churches.
- The actions of individuals.

Question Time

1 Think about how Ireland is today. Collect information about Ireland today from:
- newspapers
- TV
- radio
- the Internet.

Now answer these questions.

a Are there still problems between different groups?

b Is there still violence on the streets?

Explain your answers. Then make a factfile called 'Ireland today'.

2 Work in groups to present the things your have all found out about Ireland today. Think about the best way to present your findings. It could be:
- a wall display
- a short drama
- a TV interview
- a website.

Make your presentation to the rest of the class.

Unit 18: Hot war, cold war – why did the major twentieth-century conflicts affect so many people?

INTRODUCTION

There were many minor wars during the twentieth century. But there were three major ones. These were:

- the First World War
- the Second World War
- the Cold War.

The First and Second World Wars were 'hot' wars, where fighting happened. The Cold War was 'cold' because war was never actually declared between the two main enemies. These two enemies were the USA and the USSR.

These three wars were 'major' wars because they involved, in one way or another, most people in the world. Women were organised into war work. Children were evacuated (moved) to live in safer places. Men, women and children were bombed in their own homes. In fact, People developed bombs that were powerful enough to destroy the whole world.

People were also made poorer by wars and conflicts. Many had to escape and live in other countries as refugees. People were weakened by starvation and famine. Governments spent huge amounts of money on weapons that could have been spent on improving the lives of the people.

Activity Time

❶ Think about war.
a Talk to the person next to you about what the word 'war' means.
b Write down a definition of the word 'war'.
c Now use a dictionary to look up 'war'.
d Which definition is best? Yours, or the dictionary's? Explain why.

❷ Collect some images of war. You can get them from:
- newspapers
- magazines
- books
- the Internet.

Try to find images of war like the ones in this unit, to show the many different ways that war affects people.

WHAT HAPPENED IN TWENTIETH-CENTURY WARFARE?

Think about how wars were fought and how people were affected.

SOURCE 1

The bombing of London during the Second World War, December 1940.

SOURCE 2

A woman war worker in a munitions factory, where weapons were made during the Second World War.

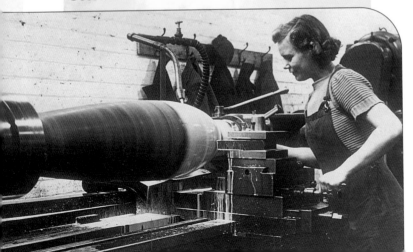

SOURCE 3

The war in Sierra Leone brought us to Liberia. The war was very serious. There was gunfire everywhere. I fled with nothing. I was running and carrying one of the children. But my other child was shot. He was six years-old. So many people died in our village, no one is left there now. Everyone fled for their lives.

In 1997, Fatima Kemokai fled from her home in Sierra Leone. This was because of a civil war that had been going on for nine years. More than one million people lost their homes. Fatima is still living as a refugee in Liberia.

SOURCE 4

Between 1981 and 1990, women held demonstrations against putting US cruise missiles at Greenham Common in Berkshire, UK.

SOURCE 5

TAKE ACTION: The UK is one of the three top arms exporters in the world. Write to the Secretary of State for Trade and Industry. Ask him to take action now!

An Oxfam campaign, June 2000.

SOURCE 6

Kosovan refugees at a camp in Macedonia in April 1999.

SOURCE 7

Nigeria is giving everything possible to the war effort. The tin mines are making engine bearings for army lorries and for railway engines. Nigeria's cotton is used for making tropical uniforms. Nigeria's animal skins are used for making army boots and belts and flying kit for RAF pilots.

From a booklet aimed at encouraging the war effort in Nigeria during the Second World War. Nigeria was part of the British Empire at that time.

SOURCE 8

The battlefield is horrible. The corpses smell sour. Men that were killed last October lie half in swamp and half in beet fields. The legs of an Englishman stick out into a trench and a soldier hangs his rifle on them.

Part of a letter home from a German soldier fighting in France in the First World War.

SOURCE 9

During the Second World War, India supplied materials to soldiers from the Commonwealth, China and the USA as well as Indian troops. India made gifts of money, too, as well as interest-free loans.

This describes part of the war effort made by India in the Second World War.

SOURCE 10

Money spent on the Second World War by USSR, USA and UK:

USSR spent £48 billion

USA spent £85 billion

UK spent £28 billion.

What is it?

Commonwealth
Countries that used to be part of the British Empire.

SOURCE 11

Estimate of the number of people killed from five countries in the Second World War.

Country	Approximate number killed	Approximate number in military forces
Britain	0.5 million	4.5 million
USSR	20.0 million	12.0 million
USA	0.4 million	11.0 million
Germany	4.2 million	12.0 million
Japan	1.2 million	4.0 million

SOURCE 12

Japanese paratroopers marching at the Annual Defence Force Day Parade in Tokyo, 19 October 1990.

Activity Time

1 Look at Sources 1 to 12. Make a card for each source. Then, on each of these cards, write in note form:
a a brief description of the source (you can draw this part if you want to)
b what you can learn from the source about twentieth-century war.
Here's an example.

SOURCE 12

- *Big armies, marching, wearing uniform.*

- *Twentieth-century war. Well organised. Cost money. Fighting by trained specialists. Uniform makes them look important. Many soldiers involved. They look prepared for war.*

---

2 Sort your cards into different categories. But first you need to think about the categories you could make. For example, all the cards and images to do with 'civilians' could go together. You decide! You might use some images in more than one category.

3 What have you learned from your categories about war in the twentieth century? Make a list of the statements. Here are some examples.

- Twentieth-century warfare affected civilians. They:
  ○ worked in factories
  ○ worked in hospitals
  ○ worked in auxiliary services
  ○ were bombed where they lived.
- Big armies were used in twentieth-century warfare.

KILLING MACHINES: FOCUS ON WAR AND TECHNOLOGY

You will now have some ideas about what happened in twentieth-century wars. There were big changes in how wars were fought. These changes were brought about by developments in technology.

THE FIRST WORLD WAR

The First World War (1914–18) was different from any war that had gone before. For a start, nine million people died – far more than in any earlier war. This was partly because of changes in technology.

Artillery

- Artillery fired large amounts of big explosives and machine guns fired very quickly.
- To protect themselves from this, soldiers dug themselves into trenches.
- It was from these trenches that most fighting took place.

Medicine

- Developments in medicine meant that fewer soldiers died from their wounds than in any other war.
- This was the first war where more people died from fighting than from disease.

> **Two facts about Lancaster bombers**
> 1 As many as 1000 planes would fly out together on bombing raids.
> 2 They were used to drop explosives on German targets.

THE SECOND WORLD WAR

By the time of the Second World War, developments in technology changed the way the war was fought.

Aircraft

Planes could fly long distances. They flew on bombing raids. They fired at other planes. They dropped bombs on factories and ports, bridges and roads, troops and warships. This meant that more civilians than soldiers were killed.

SOURCE 13

A Lancaster bomber in flight during the Second World War.

Tanks and armoured cars

Tanks and fast armoured cars could drive over rough ground and through enemy fire. They could take vital supplies to their own armies. This meant that:

- very fast attacks were made by armoured divisions
- fighting took place far from army bases.

RADAR

RADAR stands for Radio Detecting and Ranging. A RADAR system warned if enemy planes were approaching. It was especially useful at night when the planes couldn't easily be seen. It was used in aeroplanes to find and attack targets more accurately. It also helped hunt for submarines.

Medicine

Penicillin was the first ever antibiotic. It was developed during the war. Penicillin meant than an infection could be controlled, so wounded soldiers recovered quickly.

Atomic bombs

The atomic bomb was developed during the war. It was the first bomb to use nuclear power. Two atomic bombs were dropped on Japan by the **Allies** in 1945. This brought the war there to a swift end. No atom bombs have been dropped in war since 1945.

SOURCE 14

This German tank was used in the Second World War. During the Gulf War (1991) tanks attacked the enemy, carried wounded soldiers and transported supplies.

What does it mean?

Allies

Countries who helped Britain during the First and Second World Wars.

NUCLEAR WEAPONS AND THE COLD WAR

Since the 1960s, extremely powerful nuclear weapons have been developed. These could destroy the whole world. They have changed the way people think about war and how countries prepare for the possibility of war.

- A country with nuclear weapons does not need so many soldiers.
- Powerful countries built up huge stocks of nuclear weapons to stop nuclear attacks from their enemies. 'Kill us and we'll kill you' was the message.
- This policy was called 'Mutually Assured Destruction' (MAD). It happened during the Cold War.

Activity Time

Draw a chart like the one below. Using the information on pages 105 to 108, fill in the chart with information on the weapons and technology used in each war. The grid has been started for you.

	First World War	Second World War	Cold War
Weapons	Machine guns		
Bombs			Hydrogen bombs
Medicine		Penicillin	
Technology		Radar	

DOES THE ADVANCE OF TECHNOLOGY ALWAYS MAKE A DIFFERENCE IN WARFARE?

Although many countries have the technology to destroy each other (and the world), nuclear weapons haven't been used since 1945. Instead, weapons like guns, bombers and tanks have been used. Missiles are equipped with ordinary explosives, not nuclear warheads.

SOURCE 15

In the early summer of 1994, there was a program of massacres in Rwanda. These were low-tech massacres, carried out with **machetes***. They were carried out with incredible speed. At least 800,000 people were killed in just 100 days. It was the most efficient mass killing since the atomic bombings of Hiroshima and Nagasaki.*

From *We wish to inform you that tomorrow we will be killed with our families* by Philip Gourevitch, 1999.

THE SECOND WORLD WAR: TOTAL AND GLOBAL WAR IN THE TWENTIETH CENTURY

The First World War and the Second World War were the first ever total, global wars. Nearly everyone and everywhere was affected in some way.

What is it?

Civil war in Rwanda

Rwanda is a country in central East Africa that used to be a colony of Belgium. It has two main ethnic groups, the Hutus and the Tutsi. Civil war broke out between them in 1994. After the massacres, nearly two million Rwandans fled the country and became refugees.

Machete

A very heavy knife with a big blade.

Question Time

1 Look at Source 15. Why does Philip Gourevitch say that the killing in Rwanda was 'low-tech'?

2 a What is a 'mass killing'?
b Why does Philip Gourevitch say the killing in Rwanda was 'the most efficient mass killing since the atomic bombings of Hiroshima and Nagasaki'?

3 Do groups need high-tech technology in order to kill large numbers of people? Explain your answer.

Factfile: Second World War

- More than 40 million people were killed.
- More than half of those were civilians.
- More than 20 million Russians were killed.
- Ten per cent of the people of Poland were killed during the war. Half of those killed were Jewish.
- During the war, over 11 million people had to leave their homes to escape death and war. They were called 'Displaced Persons', or refugees.
- By 1948 the total number of refugees was 46 million.
- Some European countries, like France, Poland, Denmark, Holland, Belgium and Norway, were occupied by German soldiers during the war.
- Switzerland, Sweden and Spain were European countries that stayed 'neutral' during the Second World War.

Second World War in Britain

- The Emergency Powers Act of 1940 gave the British government total power over the British people.
- Unmarried women in Britain aged between 19 and 40 were made to work for the war effort from 1941 to 1945.
- Food and clothes were rationed.
- Everyone had to carry identity cards.
- People could be sent anywhere in Britain to do war work.
- During the war, London and other big British cities were heavily bombed. This became known as the 'Blitz'. About 60,000 people were killed.
- Children in Britain were evacuated out of cities at risk from bombing. They were separated from their families and sent to safe places. These places were normally in the countryside.

Question Time

1 The Factfile on page 110 says that 'more than 40 million people were killed'. Some historians think that 50 million were killed.

a Can we be certain about how many people died?

b Explain your answer.

2 Which statement in the Factfile helps to explain why so many civilians were killed during the war?

3 The British government had much more power over people during the war.

a Can you find any statements in the Factfile to describe what the government did with this power?

b Write them down.

4 The British government used propaganda *and* laws to make sure everyone was doing something during the war. Most of this propaganda was directed at women. Why do you think this was?

5 Look at pages 101 to 111. Find evidence to show that the main wars in the twentieth century affected a lot of people. You could lay out your information like the example below.

Evidence to show that the wars affected a lot of people

My first piece of evidence is ...

My second piece of evidence is ...

STORY OF SEPARATION

For many people, war means separation from loved ones, sometimes for ever. Millions of people were killed and millions more became refugees during the twentieth century.

SOURCE 16

I was six and a half years old. I didn't really understand about Hitler. I just knew we had to get out. My mother helped me choose my clothes and toys. My whole family came to see me off. There was deathly silence on the station platform. All the parents were seeing their children off.

We had luggage labels round our necks. In England, my foster-mother made it clear to me that I was lucky to be alive. She called me her 'little Czech refugee'. She boasted in church about her good deed in taking me in. I hated being a refugee. But the children in school treated me like one of them.

This is what happened to one person during the war. The account is from *Voices of the Holocaust,* an audio collection of memories made in 1993.

Source 16 describes some of the memories of a very young Czechoslovakian Jewish girl. Her parents sent her to safety in Britain just before the Second World War began. They planned to follow her, but were not allowed to leave Czechoslovakia. Most of the young Jewish refugees who reached Britain never saw their parents again.

Question Time

1 Read Source 16. Why do you think the mother sent her child away from home?

2 What did being a refugee mean to this child?

3 Look at the Factfile on page 110.
a Does the story from Source 16 link to any statements in the Factfile?
b Try to explain your links.

4 a Can you find any statements in the Factfile about how people were separated from their friends and family during the war?
b Make a list of all the ways that people were separated.

DO THE CAUSES OF TWENTIETH-CENTURY WARS HAVE ANYTHING IN COMMON?

There were many different types of war in the twentieth century.

1 Civil wars.   2 Religious wars.
3 Wars of conquest.   4 Wars fought for independence.

Below is a list of meanings for these terms. Match the correct meaning to each term.

a Wars to gain more land.
b Wars between people of different religions.
c Wars for freedom from rule by another country.
d Wars within a country between two or more groups.

You also need to remember that wars can start for different reasons. Often there is more than one reason for the start of a war. Sometimes we can see similarities and differences in these reasons.

Why do you think it is important to examine the causes of war?

The First World War was fought between two sides.

- On one side were Britain, France, Russia and the USA.
- On the other side were Germany, Austria-Hungary and Italy.

At the start of the war, many young men felt they needed to do something for their country. They rushed to join the army and have some excitement. But the horror and cruelty of the fighting soon changed their views.

SOURCE 1

A photograph from the First World War. It shows an area known as 'No Man's Land', between the German and Allied trenches. Why do you think these areas were called 'No Man's Land'?

CAUSES OF FIRST WORLD WAR

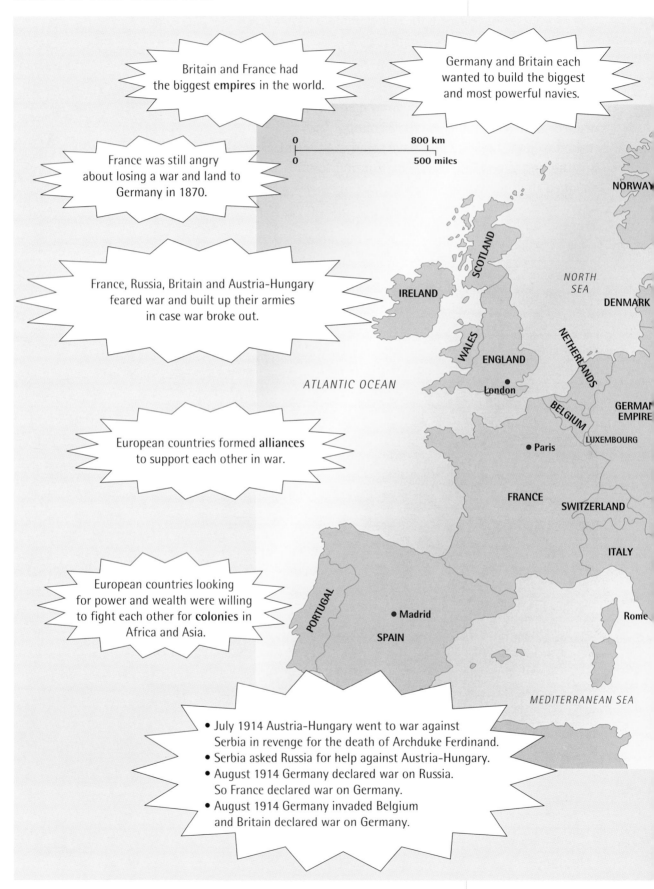

Britain and France had the biggest **empires** in the world.

Germany and Britain each wanted to build the biggest and most powerful navies.

France was still angry about losing a war and land to Germany in 1870.

France, Russia, Britain and Austria-Hungary feared war and built up their armies in case war broke out.

European countries formed **alliances** to support each other in war.

European countries looking for power and wealth were willing to fight each other for **colonies** in Africa and Asia.

- July 1914 Austria-Hungary went to war against Serbia in revenge for the death of Archduke Ferdinand.
- Serbia asked Russia for help against Austria-Hungary.
- August 1914 Germany declared war on Russia. So France declared war on Germany.
- August 1914 Germany invaded Belgium and Britain declared war on Germany.

0 ———— 800 km
0 ———— 500 miles

NORWAY

SCOTLAND

NORTH SEA

IRELAND

DENMARK

WALES

NETHERLANDS

ENGLAND

London

ATLANTIC OCEAN

BELGIUM

GERMAN EMPIRE

LUXEMBOURG

Paris

FRANCE

SWITZERLAND

ITALY

PORTUGAL

Madrid

Rome

SPAIN

MEDITERRANEAN SEA

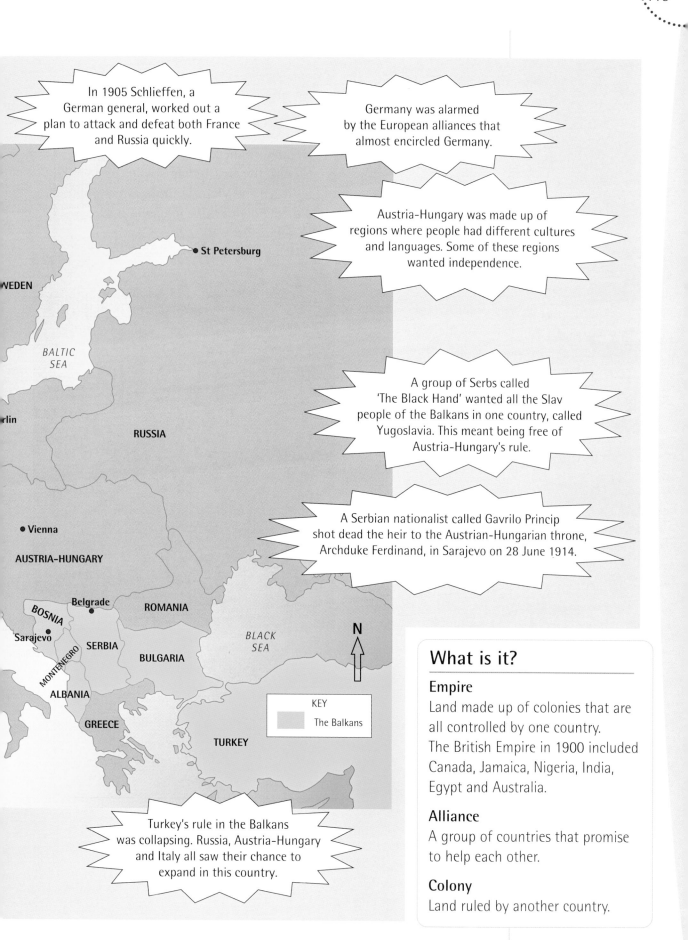

In 1905 Schlieffen, a German general, worked out a plan to attack and defeat both France and Russia quickly.

Germany was alarmed by the European alliances that almost encircled Germany.

Austria-Hungary was made up of regions where people had different cultures and languages. Some of these regions wanted independence.

A group of Serbs called 'The Black Hand' wanted all the Slav people of the Balkans in one country, called Yugoslavia. This meant being free of Austria-Hungary's rule.

A Serbian nationalist called Gavrilo Princip shot dead the heir to the Austrian-Hungarian throne, Archduke Ferdinand, in Sarajevo on 28 June 1914.

Turkey's rule in the Balkans was collapsing. Russia, Austria-Hungary and Italy all saw their chance to expand in this country.

St Petersburg
BALTIC SEA
WEDEN
rlin
RUSSIA
Vienna
AUSTRIA-HUNGARY
Belgrade
BOSNIA
ROMANIA
Sarajevo
SERBIA
MONTENEGRO
BULGARIA
BLACK SEA
ALBANIA
GREECE
TURKEY
N

KEY
The Balkans

What is it?

Empire
Land made up of colonies that are all controlled by one country. The British Empire in 1900 included Canada, Jamaica, Nigeria, India, Egypt and Australia.

Alliance
A group of countries that promise to help each other.

Colony
Land ruled by another country.

Activity Time

1 Work in small groups. Look at pages 114 to 115. Share out the causes of the war between your group. Each person in the group copies their cause on to a separate card. Decide whether the card you have is mainly about:

- freedom
- power
- revenge.

Write your decision on your card.

2 Stay in your groups.
- Take it in turns to explain how your card is a major cause of the war.
- You must try to convince others in your group that 'your' cause is the main one.

3 Still in your groups, organise your cards differently. Sort them into:
- tensions – long-standing problems between countries
- trends – ways in which the world was changing
- triggers – what made the war start when it did, and not sooner or later.

4 The conflict of 1914–18 was a *world* war. Look at the causes again and find those that help to explain why it was a *world* war.

5 Source 2 shows a painting from another side of the world. How does this painting help to explain that this was a world war?

SOURCE 2

A painting of Naik Darwan Sing. He is leading a bayonet charge against German soldiers in November 1914. He was the first Indian soldier to be awarded the Victoria Cross, which is a medal given to people who are very brave.

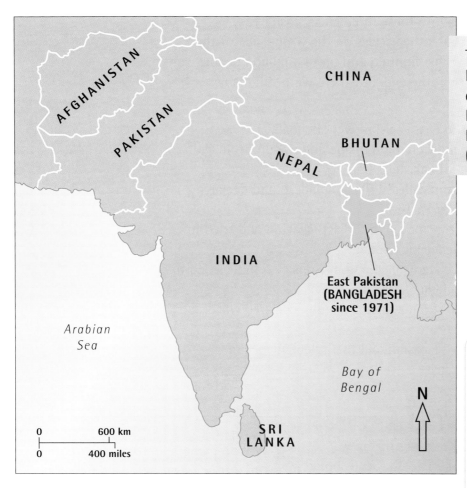

This map shows how British India was divided into Pakistan, India and East Pakistan (Bangladesh).

INDIA–PAKISTAN WAR

In 1971, India and Pakistan went to war against each other. Why? To answer this question we have to go back to 1946.

- In 1946, India and Pakistan were both part of British India.
- British and Indian politicians talked about what sort of government India should have when it broke away from the British Empire and became independent.
- There were more Hindus than **Muslims** in British India.
- Some Muslims were afraid that a **Hindu** government would not be fair to Muslim people. They wanted a country of their own.

In 1947, when India became independent, two separate countries of India and Pakistan were created. Pakistan was made up of two areas – Pakistan and East Pakistan (Bangladesh). Most Hindus lived in India. Most Muslims lived in Pakistan and East Pakistan (Bangladesh).

Who were they?

Muslims

- Muslims believe in one God, Allah.
- They believe that the greatest prophet of all ancient prophets was Muhammad.
- Muhammad was the founder of Islam in 600 AD.
- Islam is the Muslim religion.

Hindus

- Hindus worship God in many different forms.
- Hindus believe they are born again many times.
- Hinduism is India's main religion.
- Its scriptures are thousands of years old.

Dividing up British India into these three areas wasn't easy. Thousands of people found themselves on the wrong side of the frontiers. There was terrible fighting and up to a million people were killed. There was peace in the end. But there were still many problems.

- The people living in East Pakistan were Bengali.
- The Bengalis had a different language and culture from the people in the rest of Pakistan.
- In 1971, East Pakistan called itself Bangladesh and declared itself independent of Pakistan.
- So the Pakistani army moved in to East Pakistan and tried to stop the independence movement.
- Hundreds of people were killed and millions of refugees fled to India, where many Bengalis lived.
- The prime minister of India, Indira Gandhi, declared war on Pakistan.
- India soon defeated Pakistan and the independence of Bangladesh was official.

Activity Time

1 Make a list of the causes of the war between India and Pakistan. You should have no more than six causes. Write each cause on a separate card.

2 Decide whether each card is about:
- freedom
- power
- revenge, or
- fear.

3 Write a paragraph explaining what the war between India and Pakistan was all about.

SOME TWENTIETH CENTURY CONFLICTS

These are some of the main conflicts in the twentieth century.

Russian Civil War (1918–21)

White Russians were Russians who opposed the communist revolution. Red Russians were Russians who had made the revolution. The Whites fought against the Reds. British, French and American troops fought with the Whites.

Arab–Israeli conflicts (beginning 1948)

In 1948, the state of Israel was created. All the neighbouring Arab countries, including Palestine, were against this. Egypt, Syria, Jordan, Iraq and the Lebanon all attacked Israel. The Israelis defeated them all.

Korean War (1950–3)

At the end of the Second World War, separate governments were set up in North and South Korea. War broke out between them. The USSR and communist China supported North Korea. The USA and United Nations troops fought on the side of South Korea. In 1953, a truce was declared. Korea was divided into the communist North and the **capitalist** South.

Vietnam War (1964–73)

War broke out between communist North Vietnam and anti-communist South Vietnam. China supported North Vietnam and the USA supported South Vietnam. Eventually the USA withdrew, and North and South Vietnam signed a peace treaty.

The Falklands War (1982)

Britain had occupied the Falkland Islands since 1833. In 1982, Argentina claimed the islands were theirs, and sent soldiers to occupy them. The British government sent the navy to get the islands back.

Gulf War (1990–1)

Saddam Hussein, the ruler of Iraq, invaded the oil-rich country of Kuwait. Kuwait's oil was extremely important to the western world. Many countries, including Britain and the USA, went to war to free Kuwait. Iraq surrendered after a bombing campaign.

What does it mean?

Capitalist
Where money is used to make a political system work.

Activity Time

Draw a chart like the one below. Call it: **Twentieth-century wars**. Make the boxes big enough for all the information you want to include. You could do this as a whole class, putting the chart where everyone can see it and add something to it. The idea of the chart is to see easily what happened during all these wars. You will be able to compare one war with another. You will also be able to see how things changed during the twentieth century.

WAR	CAUSES: Why did the war happen?	NATURE: How was the war fought?	IMPACT: How were people and places affected in the short term?	EFFECTS: How were people and places affected in the long term?
First World War (1914–18)	Rivalry over the size of empires	Trench warfare	9 million died	
Second World War (1939–45)		Mobile: fast and far reaching		Many refugees in Europe
Cold War				
???				

You will add things to your chart as you do your research and continue your work through this unit. You should be able to fill in the bits about the First and Second World Wars and the India–Pakistan War.

Then you can decide which conflict or conflicts you or your group are going to research. Start by finding out the causes. You can use the cause-sorting exercise you did on pages 116 and 118 to help you.

WHY DID THE END OF THE SECOND WORLD WAR HAVE THE EFFECT OF STARTING ANOTHER, DIFFERENT WORLD CONFLICT?

We have looked at the causes of some 'hot' wars. Now we are going to look at how the Cold War started. Look back to page 108 to remind yourself about nuclear weapons.

SOURCE 1

Hiroshima after the bomb was dropped on 6 August 1945.

MASS KILLING IN HIROSHIMA

On 6 August 1945 an American B-29 bomber, the *Enola Gay*, dropped an atomic bomb on the city of Hiroshima in Japan. 120,000 people were killed. 78,000 were injured. Three days later, a second atomic bomb was dropped on the Japanese city of Nagasaki, killing about 74,000 people.

On 15 August 1945, Japan surrendered and the Second World War ended.

SOURCE 2

A watch that stopped the moment the bomb exploded above Hiroshima. It belonged to Kengo Futagawa, who was killed.

SOURCE 3

One effect of the radiation sickness caused by the bombs was that people lost their hair. This hair belonged to Hiroko Yamashita, who was eighteen at the time.

Question Time

1 Look at Sources 1 to 3.

a Describe these sources in your own words.

b From your descriptions, write one paragraph that explains the impact of the atomic bombs on Hiroshima and Nagasaki.

2 The things shown in Sources 2 and 3 are kept in a museum. Why would people today want to remember what happened to Hiroshima and Nagasaki in 1945?

HIROSHIMA: A CONTROVERSIAL DECISION

Did the use of atomic bombs kill fewer people than might have been killed fighting to bring the war to an end?

SOURCE 4

It would take until the autumn of 1946 to defeat Japan. General Marshall told me that half a million American troops might die. I never had any doubt that we should drop the atomic bomb. I wanted it to be dropped on a military target.

This is what Harry Truman, President of the USA (1945–53), said about his decision to drop the bomb.

SOURCE 5

The Japanese were about to surrender. But it had cost $2000 million to develop the two atomic bombs. The leaders of the development team were keen for both bombs to be tested. Nagasaki was, in short, an experiment.

From the magazine *Sanity* produced by Campaign for Nuclear Disarmament (CND).

SOURCE 6

A British cartoon from the London newspaper
Evening Standard, 1960.

JAPAN WAS SEEKING PEACE **BEFORE** THE FIRST ATOM BOMB WAS DROPPED ON HIROSHIMA, ACCORDING TO DOCUMENTS JUST LEAKED TO THE U.S. PRESS.

"DON'T YOU SEE, THEY **HAD** TO FIND OUT IF IT WORKED..."

Question Time

❶ Read Source 4 carefully.
a Did President Truman think that the atomic bombs saved lives?
b Give a reason for your answer.

❷ Read Source 5.
a Does the CND think that bombs should not have been dropped on Hiroshima and Nagasaki?
b Give reasons for your answer.

❸ Look at Source 6. Do you think the artist was for or against the atomic bomb? Explain your answer.

HIROSHIMA AS A MESSAGE TO THE USSR

The USA and the USSR fought on the same side in the Second World War. But by 1945 they were beginning to be suspicious of each other. This led to a 'cold war' that was to last for 40 years.

HIROSHIMA AS THE START OF THE ARMS RACE

Stalin ordered Soviet scientists to develop their own atomic bomb. What happened then?

- In 1949 the USSR tested its first atomic bomb in Siberia.
- In 1952 the USA tested the more powerful hydrogen bomb.
- In 1953 the USSR tested their first hydrogen bomb.
- Each side raced to get ahead of the other one.

HIROSHIMA AND PEACE

From 1945 onwards, the world knew it had the power to destroy itself. Hiroshima and Nagasaki became symbols of peace movements. A flame of peace was lit from the fires of Nagasaki. It is still alight in Japan today.

WHAT WAS THE COLD WAR? HOW DID IT START?

The Cold War began as soon as the Second World War ended. It was 'fought' between two sides.

- The USA and its allies were on one side.
- The USSR and its allies were on the other side.

It was called the Cold War because neither side actually attacked each other. On pages 125 to 128, we will find out how they did 'fight'.

Who was he?

Joseph Stalin
Dictator of Soviet Russia (USSR) from 1924 to 1953.

What was it?

Arms race
A 'race' to see which country could get the most weapons.

The USA and the USSR had different ideas and beliefs about the best way for people to live. We call these sets of beliefs 'ideologies'. Once the enemy, Germany, had been defeated, the differences in the ideologies between the USA and the USSR became dangerously clear. Read these two different ideas about what 'democracy' meant.

USA: THE CAPITALISTS

We are democratic! We believe that all people should be equal and free. Our whole political system is based on these things. People are free to vote for the rulers of their choice. There are at least two political parties. And governments can only be in power for a limited time. People are also free to own property, voice their opinions and move around as they want to.

USSR: THE COMMUNISTS

We are democratic! We believe that all people should be equal and free. We believe that they cannot be free until they are equal. Otherwise freedom is just for the rich. Under our system there is no private ownership of property. Instead, the state owns everything. It uses what it has to look after the Russian people. It gives them jobs, health care and housing. People can vote for the one political party that will truly take care of their interests.

SOURCE 7

This is a Russian cartoon entitled 'Land of the free'. It is about the political system of the USA.

Activity Time

1 Read the statements opposite.
a Sort them out into 'capitalist' and 'communist' statements.
b Make a chart like the one below.
c Write the statements into the correct column.

- Governments are chosen from one political party.
- People can be told what jobs to do and where to live.
- People can buy their own property.
- People can move around as they want.
- Governments are elected by people who have a choice of political parties to vote for.
- All property is owned by the state.

COMMUNIST	CAPITALIST

2 Work in pairs. One of you will be a 'communist' and will pretend that you prefer the ideas of this system. One of you will be a 'capitalist' and pretend that you prefer these ideas. Try to convince your partner that your system is better. To help, you and your partner could discuss the questions opposite, then make some notes.

- How do people get jobs?
- How do people find houses to live in?
- Are there very rich and very poor people in your country?
- How fair is your system of government?
- Are people free?
- Are people equal?

WHY DID THE COLD WAR START WHEN IT DID?

The differences in ideologies between the USSR and the USA had existed since the USSR became communist in 1922. After 1945, there were other reasons for tensions.

PROBLEMS OF PEACE

At the end of a war, there are always new problems to be solved.

- How should the losers be treated?
- How were countries to rebuild after the devastation of war?
- Who would pay for the damage?
- What would happen to refugees?

These were the questions that faced the world in 1945. There were no easy answers. In trying to solve these problems, the relationship between the USA and USSR worsened. The two countries became more and more suspicious of each other. As you read the timeline, try to work out why.

Timeline: USA and USSR 1945–49

1945
- **February** Peace talks at Yalta.
- **July** Peace talks at Potsdam.
- USSR supports communist government in Yugoslavia.

1946
- **March** 'Iron Curtain' speech by Winston Churchill.
- USSR sets up communist governments in Albania and Bulgaria.

1947
- USSR sets up communist governments in Poland and Romania.
- **Truman Doctrine** – USA says it will help people everywhere resist communism.
- **Marshall Plan** – USA gives money to non-communist countries in western Europe to help them defend themselves against communism.

1948
- Communists seize power in Czechoslovakia.
- USSR cuts off Berlin from the West. Berlin Airlift sends in supplies.

1949
- German Federal Republic (West Germany) set up by the USA and its allies.
- USSR turns eastern Germany into the German Democratic Republic (East Germany).

This map shows the spread of Soviet influence in eastern Europe.

NORWAY

SWEDEN

Estonia

BALTIC STATES

Latvia

DENMARK

Lithuania

NETHERLANDS

Berlin

EAST GERMANY

POLAND

SOVIET UNION

WEST GERMANY

CZECHOSLOVAKIA

FRANCE

SWITZERLAND

AUSTRIA

HUNGARY

ITALY

ROMANIA

YUGOSLAVIA

BULGARIA

Black Sea

ALBANIA

GREECE

TURKEY

Land taken by USSR at the end of Second World War

Soviet-controlled communist countries

Non-Soviet-controlled communist country

N

250 miles
400 km

THE SOVIET POINT OF VIEW

The USSR suffered terribly in the Second World War. Nearly 20 million Russian people died defending eastern Europe against Germany. Joseph Stalin was determined this would not happen again. He wanted to set up a barrier of communist states between Germany and the USSR.

SOURCE 8

This cartoon was published in the *Daily Mail*, a British newspaper. In March 1946 the British Prime Minister, Winston Churchill, talked about an 'iron curtain' falling across Europe.

PEEP UNDER THE IRON CURTAIN

Question Time

❶ You will need to use the timeline and map on page 127 to help you answer these questions.
a How did the USSR increase its influence in Europe between 1945 and 1947?
b How did the USA react to these changes?

❷ Look at Source 8.
a Who is 'Joe' in the cartoon?
b Why does the notice say 'No admittance'?
c What messages are being sent about eastern Europe and western Europe?

❸ Turn back to page 120. Look again at the chart you made on twentieth-century wars. You can now add some ideas and information to the 'Causes' column for the Cold War.

FORTY YEARS OF COLD WAR?

On pages 129 to 135 you will find out about four incidents in the Cold War. But how did the USA and USSR 'fight' the Cold War? They both:

- supported possible friendly countries with money and weapons
- used military strength (especially nuclear weapons) to threaten possible enemies
- tried to control the governments of other countries
- used spies and surveillance techniques
- mistrusted each other
- competed to appear the most powerful to the rest of the world
- never declared war on each other.

1 BERLIN AIRLIFT 1948–9

For ten months in 1948–9, planes carrying everything from saucepans to sausages flew in to Berlin. It was the only way everyday life in the western part of the city could carry on. How had this happened?

- After the Second World War, Germany was divided up between France, the USA, Britain and the USSR.
- Berlin was divided in the same way. But the city was in the part of Germany run by the USSR.
- Westerners could only reach Berlin by going through Soviet-controlled Germany.
- By 1949, the parts of Germany run by the USA, France and Britain had joined together. The Soviet sector stayed separate.
- The Soviet sector became communist.

This map shows the air corridor routes for planes flying goods from West Germany into West Berlin.

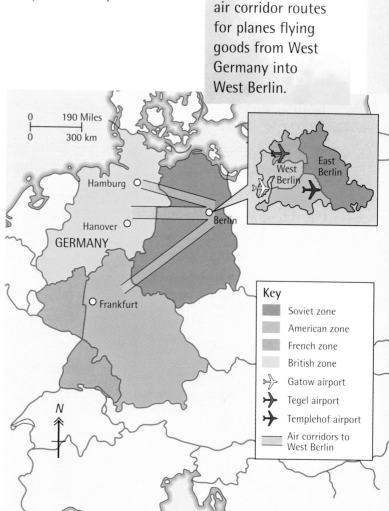

0 — 190 Miles
0 — 300 km

Hamburg

Hanover
GERMANY

Berlin

West Berlin · East Berlin

Frankfurt

N

Key

- Soviet zone
- American zone
- French zone
- British zone
- Gatow airport
- Tegel airport
- Templehof airport
- Air corridors to West Berlin

Because of the Marshall Plan (see the timeline on page 127), capitalist West Germany made a good recovery from the war. But communist East Germany did not.

Stalin, the leader of the USSR, was suspicious of what the western countries were doing. In June 1948 he cut road, rail and canal links with West Germany. Berlin was isolated in communist East Germany. But the USA, France and Britain were determined to keep control of their zones in Berlin. They flew essential supplies into the city, hour by hour, day by day.

Finally, in May 1949, the USSR gave up and links with West Germany were opened again.

The Berlin Wall

In the 1960s, **Khrushchev** said he wanted Soviet control of Berlin. In August 1961, he ordered a wall to be built to divide East and West Berlin. Within two weeks, this had been done.

Question Time

❶ Why do you think Stalin cut off all links between communist East Germany and capitalist West Germany?

❷ The USSR did not try to shoot down any planes during the Berlin Airlift. What does this tell you about the Cold War?

❸ Look back to the list of characteristics of the Cold War. Which ones are relevant to the Berlin Airlift?

2 HUNGARY 1956: A HOLE IN THE IRON CURTAIN?

In 1956, there was an uprising in Hungary against Soviet rule. Many who rebelled were students and young people. At first the rebellion was successful. A new and less extreme government was set up. Hungarians began to enjoy freedoms they had not had for years.

But the USSR was afraid that rebellion would spread to other communist countries in eastern Europe. Khrushchev ordered Soviet troops in to Hungary and for ten days there was fierce street fighting. Hungarians pleaded for help from the West, but none came. The Soviets set up strict measures and 200,000 Hungarians fled abroad.

Who was he?

Nikita Khrushchev
Prime Minister in the USSR from 1958 to 1964.

Question Time

1 Look at the map on page 127. Explain why the break away of Hungary from Soviet control would make a 'hole' in the Iron Curtain.

2 Why were the Soviets so keen to repair the curtain?

3 Look back to page 129.
   a Re-read the list of characteristics of the Cold War.
   b List which characteristics are relevant to Hungary in 1956.

4 Some children as young as ten years old died fighting against the USSR in Hungary. Are there any causes for which you would risk your life?

3 COMMUNISTS IN THE USA'S BACK YARD! THE CUBAN MISSILE CRISIS, 1962

The Cuban missile crisis of 1962 caused fear and panic throughout the world. Many people thought nuclear war was going to break out.

This map shows the major towns and cities in the USA that were in the range of nuclear missiles based in Cuba.

|ı|ı| Soviet missile bases
----- US naval blockade

CANADA

Seattle

Minneapolis · Detroit

San Francisco · Salt Lake City · Boston

Los Angeles · Denver · Chicago · Pitts-burgh · New York

U S A · Kansas City · Washington

Santa Fé · Oklahoma City · Louisville

Dallas · Nashville · Atlantic Ocean

New Orleans

Tampa

Havana

CUBA

1000 km range from Cuba

2500 km range from Cuba

2000 km range from Cuba

Pacific Ocean

MEXICO

N

621 miles

1000 km

'COUNTDOWN TO THE END OF THE WORLD?'

1959		Fidel Castro, a communist, takes over power in Cuba.
1961	April	A small USA force lands at the Bay of Pigs in Cuba. It hopes to stir up a revolution against Castro. There is no uprising and the USA force is easily defeated. Khrushchev supplies weapons to Cuba.
1962	16 October	US spy planes take photographs of Cuba. These photos show launch pads for long-range nuclear missiles. Photographs of Soviet ships sailing to Cuba show missiles on their decks.
	22 October	President John Kennedy of the USA orders a naval blockade of Cuba to stop the Russian ships getting through. Kennedy says that if the blockade is forced, it will be war. Soviet ships carry on sailing to Cuba.
	24 October	Soviet ships stop when they reach the blockade.
	26 October	Khrushchev says he will not put long-range missiles on Cuba if Kennedy ends the blockade. Kennedy agrees.
	28 October	All missile bases are removed from Cuba and the American blockade is lifted.

Do nothing. Allow missiles to land on Cuba and hope that they are never fired.

Attack the Soviet ships sailing towards Cuba.

Attack Cuba with nuclear weapons and destroy the missile launch sites.

Try to stop missiles reaching Cuba by setting up a naval blockade.

Activity Time

1 Work in pairs. Look at the drawing of President Kennedy and the four choices he had to solve the Cuban Missile Crisis.

a Make a list of the advantages of each choice.

b Make a list of the disadvantages of each choice.

You could put the information on a chart like the one below.

	Advantages	Disadvantages
Choice 1		
Choice 2		

2 We know that President Kennedy chose to try to stop the missiles reaching Cuba by setting up a naval blockade. Does this mean that any of the other choices would have led to war? Explain your answer.

3 Why was there an international crisis over Cuba? Write a short explanation, using:
- the map on page 131
- the timeline on page 132
- what you know about nuclear weapons.

4 Why do you think nuclear war didn't break out in October 1962?

4 THE 'GREAT POWERS' AND AFGHANISTAN

In 1979, the communist Afghan government felt threatened by Islamic (Muslim) rebels. The government was afraid that the rebels would join up with Muslims in the USSR and set up a Muslim state in Afghanistan. The USSR was afraid that the Soviet Muslims would break away to join the Afghan rebels. So the USSR sent troops in to Afghanistan to support the government there.

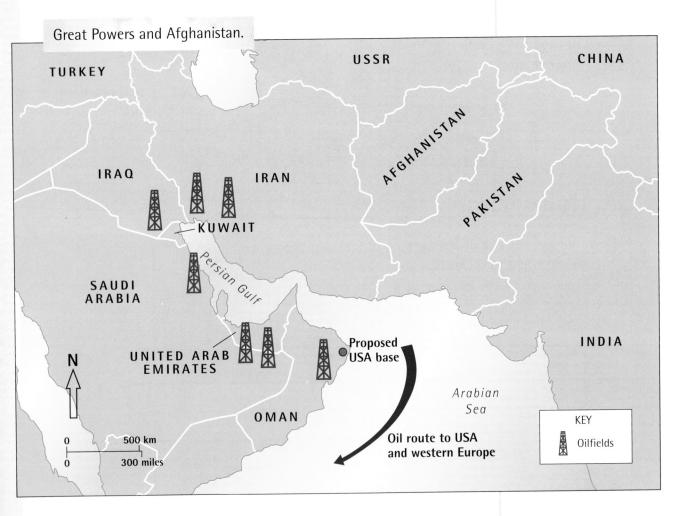

Great Powers and Afghanistan.

Question Time

❶ Look at the map above. Then answer these questions.
a Why would the USSR be interested in who has control in Afghanistan?
b Why would the USA be interested in who rules Afghanistan?

Why was the USA interested in what the USSR was doing in Afghanistan?

- Soviet troops were getting close to the oil fields of Iran, Iraq and Saudi Arabia.
- Oil is an extremely important resource for the West.

What did the USA do?

- It stopped selling food to the USSR.
- It sent soldiers to support the Muslim Afghan rebels.
- It withdrew athletes from the Moscow Olympic Games.

Soviet troops finally left Afghanistan in February 1989.

Activity Time

Whose side was China on in the war in Afghanistan?

Work in groups of three. Each of you will pretend to be advisers to Deng Xiaoping, the leader of China. Deng wants you all to give him advice about whose side China should be on in the war in Afghanistan.

Factfile: China

- China and the USSR had different kinds of communism. They were suspicious of each other.
- China and the USSR wanted to increase their influence in the world.
- China supplied weapons to Bangladesh, an Islamic country that supported the Afghan rebels.
- China and the USSR were arguing over where their borders were.
- China and the USSR supported different sides in civil wars in Korea, Vietnam and Cambodia.

You must decide before you meet with him what you will say. Study the Factfile above. Then discuss what advice you will give Deng about which side to join.

USE OF PROPAGANDA

Propaganda was an important 'weapon' in the Cold War. Look at Sources 9 and 10. Try to work out whether these cartoons are anti-Soviet or anti-USA propaganda. How did you decide? Turn back to page 120. Look again at the chart you made on twentieth-century wars. You should now have ideas and information to add to the Nature and Impact columns of the Cold War.

SOURCE 9

'Who's next to be liberated from freedom?'

" WHO'S NEXT TO BE LIBERATED FROM FREEDOM, COMRADE ?"

SOURCE 10

A cartoon from 1950 showing arms reaching from The White House, where the President of the USA lives.

HOW DID THE COLD WAR END?

DÉTENTE

The word 'détente' means 'relaxing'. From the end of the 1960s, the USSR and the USA looked for ways of relaxing the tensions of the Cold War.

Both countries had realised that far too much money was being spent on weapons. This money would be better spent on industry, agriculture and welfare at home.

'STAR WARS'

In the 1980s, the President of the USA, Ronald Reagan, started a 'Star Wars' programme. This aimed to set up an anti-missile system in space. Reagan hated communists and was determined to win the arms race. The USSR and the USA built up more and more deadly and accurate nuclear weapons.

ENTER MIKHAIL GORBACHEV

Mikhail Gorbachev became leader of the USSR in 1985. He persuaded President Reagan to begin talking about limiting the number of weapons held by both sides.

Gorbachev had two main policies.

- *Perestroika* – improving the economy to raise the standard of living.
- *Glasnost* – greater openness with the West, including the USA.

Gorbachev met many western leaders and talked about how to end the Cold War. His policies encouraged many people in eastern Europe to challenge and overthrow their governments.

Gorbachev and Reagan began to talk about limiting the number of nuclear weapons in the USA and USSR.

THE WALL COMES DOWN!

Source 1 shows the scenes in Berlin when the Berlin Wall came down in November 1989. Source 2 describes what happened in Romania in 1989 when the communist dictator Ceausescu was overthrown by the people.

SOURCE 1

These Berliners were reunited for the first time in 28 years.

SOURCE 2

On 21 December 1989, Ceausescu spoke to a rally in Bucharest (Romania). To his astonishment, his speech was interrupted by shouts from the crowd.

On the morning of 22 December, he made a final attempt to speak to the crowd. They shouted him down with cries of 'Death! Death!' The troops made no attempt to stop them.

Ceausescu and his wife were airlifted from the roof of the building just as demonstrators broke in. Both the US and Soviet governments said they were in support of the revolution against Ceausescu.

Nicholae and Elena Ceausescu were put on trial. They were found guilty of:

- mass murder
- corruption
- the destruction of the economy.

They were condemned to death and executed by a firing squad.

From Keesing's *Contemporary Archives*, December 1989.

Question Time

1 According to Source 2, Ceausescu was astonished to be interrupted during his speech. What does this tell us about how he ruled before December 1989?

2 The army did not help Ceausescu.
a Why would losing their support be so terrible?
b Why do you think the army commanders did not support him?

Timeline: The Cold War

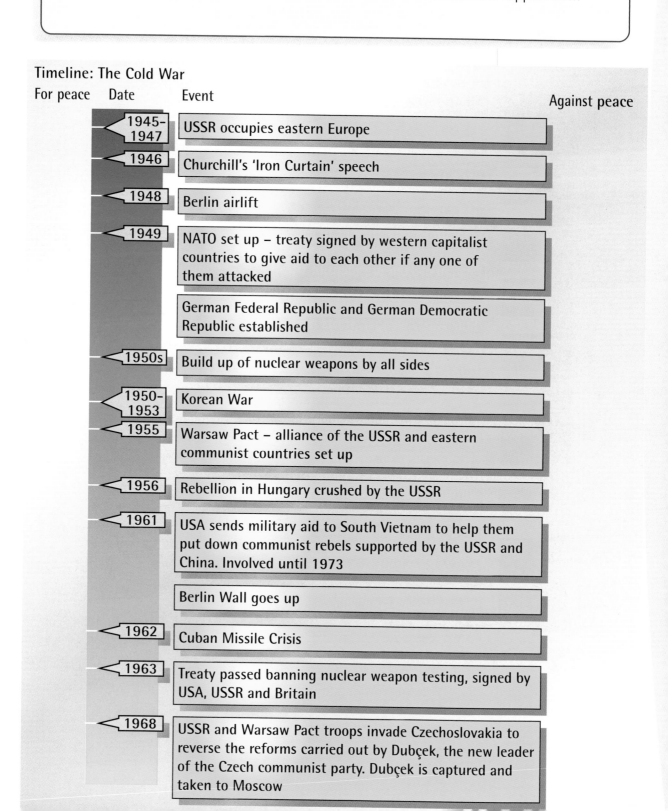

For peace	Date	Event	Against peace
	1945–1947	USSR occupies eastern Europe	
	1946	Churchill's 'Iron Curtain' speech	
	1948	Berlin airlift	
	1949	NATO set up – treaty signed by western capitalist countries to give aid to each other if any one of them attacked	
		German Federal Republic and German Democratic Republic established	
	1950s	Build up of nuclear weapons by all sides	
	1950–1953	Korean War	
	1955	Warsaw Pact – alliance of the USSR and eastern communist countries set up	
	1956	Rebellion in Hungary crushed by the USSR	
	1961	USA sends military aid to South Vietnam to help them put down communist rebels supported by the USSR and China. Involved until 1973	
		Berlin Wall goes up	
	1962	Cuban Missile Crisis	
	1963	Treaty passed banning nuclear weapon testing, signed by USA, USSR and Britain	
	1968	USSR and Warsaw Pact troops invade Czechoslovakia to reverse the reforms carried out by Dubçek, the new leader of the Czech communist party. Dubçek is captured and taken to Moscow	

Timeline: The Cold War

| For peace | Date | Event | | Against peace |

| Late 1960s | The beginning of Détente |

| 1972 | SALT 1 (Strategic Arms Limitation Talks) USSR and USA agree to limit nuclear weapons |

| 1975 | Helsinki Agreement – USA, USSR, Canada and most European countries accept European frontiers drawn up after the Second World War. Soviet dominance recognised in eastern Europe. All countries agree to recognise human rights, including freedom to leave a country |

| | American and Soviet astronauts meet in space |

| 1979 | USSR invades Afghanistan |

| 1980 | USA gives support to right-wing rebels against the communist government in Nicaragua |

| 1981 | Reagan elected president of the USA, and doubles amount of money spent on defence |

| 1984 | 'Star Wars'. Reagan starts programme of anti-missile system in space |

| 1985 | Gorbachev becomes leader of the USSR |

| 1986 | Gorbachev introduces policy of *Glasnost*, meaning greater openness with the west |

| 1987 | Treaty signed between USA and USSR agreeing to withdraw missiles from Europe |

| 1989 | Berlin Wall comes down |

| | Soviet troops leave Afghanistan |

| | Eastern European countries end Soviet domination of governments |

Activity Time

① Since 1949 some events have made the Cold War seem as if it was against peace. Other events have made peace seem quite likely. Some events might have seemed as if they were both against peace and for it.
a Look at the timeline on pages 139 and 140.
b Decide which events might have been 'for peace' and discuss why.
c Decide which events might have been 'against peace' and discuss why.

② Turn back to page 120. Look again at the chart you made on twentieth-century wars. You should now be able to add much more information to the Impact and Effect columns of the Cold War.

WHAT DO LOCAL PEOPLE REMEMBER ABOUT THE MAIN CONFLICTS?

What people remember of war depends very much on how they
were affected. Let's use Britain as an example. During the First and Second World Wars we can see that:

- some areas were bombed
- some areas took in refugees from other parts of the world
- all areas sent men to fight and die
- women in all areas were involved in the war effort.

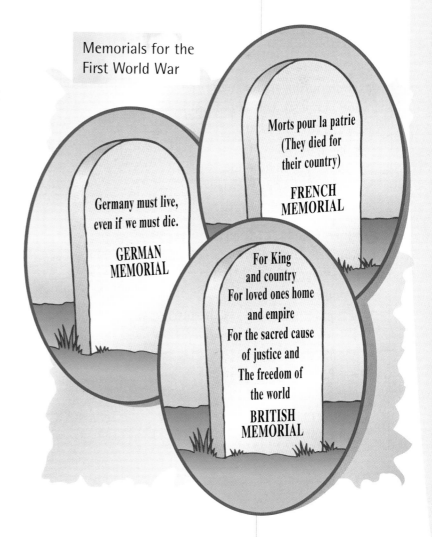

Memorials for the First World War

Morts pour la patrie
(They died for their country)

FRENCH MEMORIAL

Germany must live, even if we must die.

GERMAN MEMORIAL

For King and country
For loved ones home and empire
For the sacred cause of justice and
The freedom of the world

BRITISH MEMORIAL

WHY DID THE MAJOR TWENTIETH-CENTURY
CONFLICTS AFFECT SO MANY PEOPLE?

Activity Time

1 Look at the three national memorials on page 141. They are all from the First World War. What reasons do the memorials give for the deaths of soldiers in the First World War?

You can put the information on to a chart like the one below, if you like.

Country of memorial	Reason for deaths of the soldiers
German	
French	
British	

2 Find your local war memorial, and see if you can visit it. If you are not sure where it is, you can:
• ask your teacher
• look at a local map
• ask a friend or relative
• check at your library.

3 When you are at the memorial, make notes on the following.
a The war (or wars) that it commemorates.
b The actual words on the memorial.
• Does the memorial explain how people died?
• What reason does it give?
c The names on it.
• How many seem to be from the same family?

4 **a** Make a collage of pictures about war. Call it 'What war means to me'. It is important that the collage properly represents your own feelings about war.
• You may choose pictures and photographs from this book.
• You can also choose them from other places – for example, other books, newspapers and magazines.
b Pin all the collages around your classroom walls. Talk about why they are different.

5 Look at the spidergram on page 143. It shows how different people in the world – the Hungarian people, the American people and the Soviet people – were affected by different aspects of different wars.
a Choose three more peoples to fill the empty spaces.
b Write down how those peoples were affected by conflict.

Factfile

The Commonwealth War Graves Commission
This organisation looks after all the war graves of British and Commonwealth people who die in war overseas.

- Visit their website and find your way around it.
- Now chose one of the names on your local war memorial. Use the website to find out as much as you can about this person.

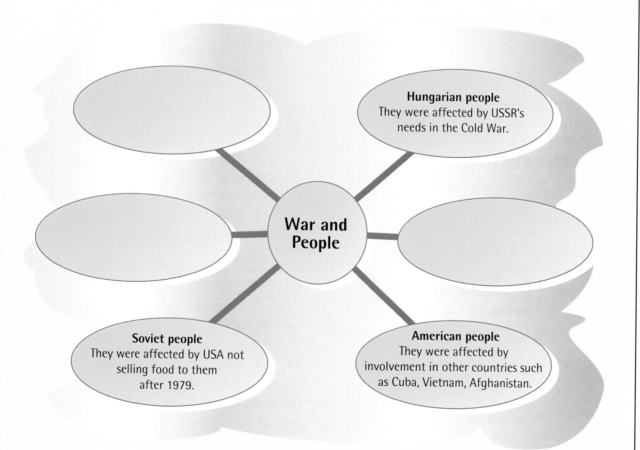

Hungarian people
They were affected by USSR's needs in the Cold War.

War and People

Soviet people
They were affected by USA not selling food to them after 1979.

American people
They were affected by involvement in other countries such as Cuba, Vietnam, Afghanistan.

Unit 19: How and why did the Holocaust happen?

RIGHTS AND RESPONSIBILITIES?

The Holocaust is the word used for the deliberate murder of over six million Jews in Europe between 1933 and 1945. Adolf Hitler's Nazi Party killed other people as well as Jews. These other people included gypsies, homosexuals and the mentally ill.

But Hitler especially wanted to wipe out the whole of the Jewish people. This story is an upsetting one. We ask why the Holocaust happened at all.

The Jewish people had no rights to protect themselves from the Nazi Party. Do you know what rights you have in society today? This is the start of our investigation.

THE UNIVERSAL DECLARATION OF HUMAN RIGHTS – THE EXAMPLE FOR THE MODERN WORLD

In 1948 the United Nations drew up a list of rights that every human in the world should have. This is called the Universal Declaration of Human Rights. It is a list of rules to protect people. Every country should follow it. It includes the rights to life, freedom, education and freedom of religion.

Question Time

❶ a Find a copy of your school mission statement or student charter.
b Read through the statement or charter, and underline the key words that show your rights.

❷ In school, like in society, we have responsibilities as well as rights. These are things we should do to make society or school work well. Copy these spider diagrams and add your own ideas. Use your notes from Question 1 for help.

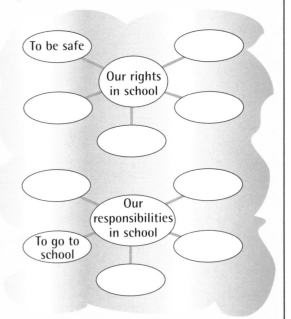

❸ a Look up the words 'universal' and 'declaration' in a dictionary.
b Now test your partner to see if they understand why the United Nations list of human rights was called a 'universal declaration'.

You will find the Declaration on page 97. We take most of its ideas for granted. But groups like Amnesty International check that people all over the world are taking notice of human rights.

THE PROTECTION OF RIGHTS

Our society is democratic. It thinks that everyone should have an equal say. We are protected in society in several ways.

- We have laws and a Parliament to pass and change laws.
- We have a police force and judges to check that laws are being followed.
- In school there are rules and people there to protect you against violence, theft and any other problems.

IGNORING PEOPLE'S RIGHTS

On the news each day we are shown places in the world where people's rights are being ignored.

- Sometimes there is an argument over land.
- Sometimes there is an argument over who should have power.

Some countries, governments and groups do not let people have their basic rights. One example is when a government uses an army to make people agree and do as they are told.

Governments and political parties also use the media to control people's ideas. Sometimes people are not told the truth. This means that they do not have freedom of information. Taking away people's rights can also mean taking away their responsibilities so that they cannot be part of society.

Question Time

❶ Does anyone in your group know a recent news story that shows human rights being ignored? Share your ideas.

❷ How many different ways can you think of that might be used to take away people's rights? Add this to your spider diagram about rights (see page 144). Use a different colour pen. Share your ideas in a group.

❸ What basic right would you hate to lose the most? Discuss your ideas with a partner.

HOW DID NAZI PERSECUTION OF THE JEWS DEVELOP?

ANTI-JEWISH ATTITUDES IN NAZI GERMANY

There were lots of Jewish people living in Germany in the 1930s. But they were not thought of as German citizens, and did not have the same rights as other German people.

Many Jewish people had built up successful businesses and grown rich. A lot of Germans were jealous of their wealth and success, especially as Germany was poor at this time. Jewish people in Germany were thought of as outsiders. They were not popular.

The Nazi Party, led by Adolf Hitler, came to power in 1933. The Nazi government thought that the **Aryan race** should rule the world. The Nazis thought that Jews would get in the way of their success. They blamed the Jewish people for all Germany's problems.

What does it mean?

Aryan race
The Aryan race was made up of most Germans.

GERMANY'S PROBLEMS – WORLD DEPRESSION IN THE 1920s AND 30s

The effects of the First World War were debt and economic depression for Europe and the USSR. Germany was weak after losing the First World War. The problems across the world just made Germany's problems worse.

The World
- Countries are high in debt and have high unemployment.
- The USA has an economic crisis in 1929 that makes the world depression worse.

The effects of the First World War

Germany
- The Treaty of Versailles blamed Germany for the war.
- Germany had to pay compensation, hand over land and cut back its army.

Germany lost its pride and had huge debts. Money lost its value and people lost their jobs. One group, the Jews, were blamed for all Germany's problems.

ANTI-SEMITISM – AN OLD IDEA

Hitler and the Nazi Party were not the first to think of the Jews as outsiders and treat them badly. The map below shows examples of **anti-Semitism** dating back to the Middle Ages.

- Jewish people stood out as different in areas across Europe. They had a different religion and different customs when most of the population had become Christian.
- Some Christians blamed Jewish people for the execution of Jesus Christ.
- In big cities Jewish people were often forced to live together in their own areas, called ghettos.
- Some Jews became money lenders because they were banned from other work. The profits they got from this made people jealous.
- Jewish people often had to wear a yellow badge or a special hat to show them as different and to make them feel less important.
- Jewish people were often expelled from countries by some rulers.

What does it mean?

Anti-Semitism
Acting against Jewish people.

This map shows where acts of anti-Semitism took place in Europe before the twentieth century.

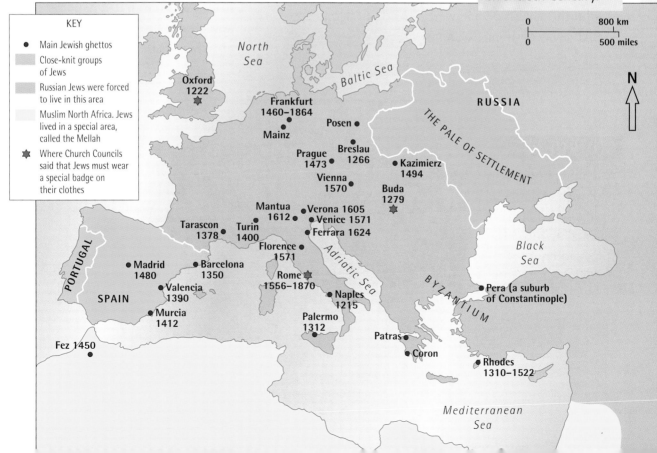

KEY

- Main Jewish ghettos
- Close-knit groups of Jews
- Russian Jews were forced to live in this area
- Muslim North Africa. Jews lived in a special area, called the Mellah
- Where Church Councils said that Jews must wear a special badge on their clothes

North Sea

Baltic Sea

RUSSIA

THE PALE OF SETTLEMENT

Oxford 1222

Frankfurt 1460–1864

Posen

Mainz

Prague 1473

Breslau 1266

Kazimierz 1494

Vienna 1570

Buda 1279

Mantua 1612

Verona 1605

Venice 1571

Ferrara 1624

Tarascon 1378

Turin 1400

Florence 1571

Adriatic Sea

Black Sea

Madrid 1480

Barcelona 1350

Rome 1556–1870

BYZANTIUM

Pera (a suburb of Constantinople)

Valencia 1390

SPAIN

Naples 1215

Murcia 1412

Palermo 1312

Patras

PORTUGAL

Fez 1450

Coron

Rhodes 1310–1522

Mediterranean Sea

N

0   800 km

0   500 miles

Question Time

❶ Why did some Church Councils make Jewish people wear special badges or hats?

❷ a Do you think that being expelled from a country and starting again in a new country would make Jewish people more accepted or less accepted?
b Give reasons for your answer.

ANTI-SEMITISM 1933–9

There is nothing unusual about the children in the photograph (Source 2). Jewish children went to school with German children. Jewish families led normal lives in German towns and cities.

After Hitler came to power, he and the Nazi Party began to make Jewish people feel different. He copied many of the actions that had been taken against Jewish people in the past. He wanted to take away their power and make the Nazi Party more powerful. The Nazis started by working out who the Jewish people were. Then they began to take away all their freedoms.

SOURCE 1

Now the Jews carry germs of the worst kind, and they infect everywhere. The Jew is a typical parasite, living at the cost of other people.

What Hitler thought about the Jewish people. This is an extract from Hitler's book *Mein Kampf* (*My Struggle*). It was written in 1924 and shows his strong anti-Semitism.

SOURCE 2

A school photograph of Jewish children in Germany. What is unusual about the children in the photograph?

German laws took away Jewish rights after Hitler became leader of Germany in 1933

1933

1 April – National boycott of Jewish shops and businesses.

6 April – Jewish people could no longer work for the government.

10 May – Jewish and anti-Nazi books were burned in public.

1935

21 May – Jews could no longer join the army.

Summer – parks, swimming baths, restaurants and public buildings were closed to Jews all over Germany.

September – the Nuremberg Laws were passed stating that no Jew could be a German citizen or vote. It was made illegal for any German to marry a Jew.

1938

23 July – Jews had to carry identity cards.

28 October – Polish Jews were taken from Germany to ghettos and work camps in Poland.

9–10 November – Kristallnacht (called 'Crystal Night' in English after all the broken glass in the streets). This was a night of violence when Jewish shops and synagogues were attacked and over 100 Jews killed.

1939

28 October – Jews in Poland had to wear yellow stars.

WINNING PEOPLE'S MINDS

The Nazi Party did not just use laws and the police against the Jewish people. Another powerful weapon was propaganda. Joseph Goebbels was Hitler's Minister of People's Enlightenment and Propaganda. He organised many different types of propaganda to make German people agree with the Nazi government.

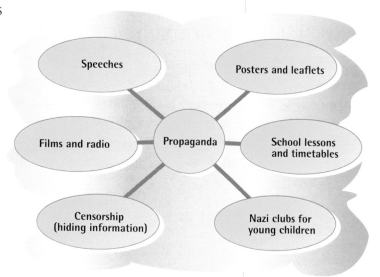

SOURCE 3

German children were taught in their school books to hate Jewish people. This cartoon shows a Jewish teacher and Jewish children being expelled from a German school.

Question Time

❶ Study Source 1. What image does Hitler give of Jewish people?

❷ Look at the timeline on page 149. In pairs discuss the following.
a The events that identified the Jewish people.
b The events that stopped them being part of German society.

❸ Study Source 3.
a How can you tell who the Jewish people are?
b What are the Jewish people doing?
c What is the message of the cartoon?
d Why was it a clever idea to spread Nazi ideas in schools in Germany?

THE SITUATION GETS WORSE – THE OUTBREAK OF WAR

- The Second World War was declared in 1939 as Germany invaded Poland.
- As Germany invaded Europe, Jews in other countries became the target for the Germans. The Nazi armies quickly brought in Hitler's anti-Semitic laws wherever they invaded.

ANTI-SEMITISM IN GERMANY AFTER 1939

In October 1939 Nazi policies changed – from identifying and controlling the Jews to planning to wipe out the whole race. Jews were used as workers to help make weapons and goods for the war. Ghettos were set up where the Jews were forced to live. The ghettos were crowded areas. They were usually near railway lines, so that the Jews could be easily moved. Jews could not leave the ghettos.

KEY
● Concentration camps

KEY
Numbers of Jews in each country based on Nazi reports
- under 10,000
- 10,000 to 50,000
- 50,000 to 100,000
- 100,000 to 500,000
- 500,000 to 1 million
- over 1 million
- figures not known

THE FINAL SOLUTION

Between 1941 and 1942 the Nazis made plans to deal with what they called the 'Jewish Problem'. These plans were called the Final Solution. Only a few top-ranking Nazis knew about the plans.

- The Final Solution was the killing of all Jewish people in Europe.
- Jews in Europe were to be rounded up and taken to large camps. There they were put to work or killed.
- In July 1941 gas was tested in Auschwitz camp in Poland as a way of killing large numbers of people.
- By December 1941 the first extermination camp was set up, also in Poland.
- By 1942 enemies of the Nazis were sent to a concentration camp or shot by mobile murder units.

Hitler's invasion of Europe.
- The top map shows the number of Jews in each country, based on Nazi reports. It also shows the concentration camps.
- The lower map shows the years when Germany invaded other European countries.

Question Time

1. What rights and responsibilities had been taken away from the Jews by 1940? Look back at pages 149–150 for help.

2. What was the main aim of Nazi anti-Semitic policy after 1941?

3. Why did the Nazis want big extermination camps as well as mobile murder units to carry out their Final Solution?

HOW AND WHY WERE GHETTOS SET UP AND WHAT WAS IT LIKE INSIDE THEM?

Jews from country and town areas all over the new German Empire were rounded up and taken into ghettos before being sent to camps. Ghettos were set up in slum areas in large towns and cities.

SOURCE 1

A Jewish mother and her children in the Warsaw ghetto.

SOURCE 2

About 40,000 Jews were rounded up and taken into the ghetto. When I passed through the wooden gates of the ghetto, I breathed a sigh of relief, because we were no longer being herded through the streets by Germans. I thought that I had left my enemies outside. How could I know that there was only an entrance to the ghetto – no exit!

We were sent to a house that would have housed a family of four to six people.

Now 25 or 30 of us were crammed in. Everybody was looking for a place to sleep. I was lucky. My mother found an empty space under a table and that became my bed. Going to the synagogue, praying and studying about our religion were not allowed. The Germans wanted to break the Jewish spirit. Many people lost their will to live. But I was too stubborn to give in.

A survivor remembers his first days in the Vilna ghetto in Poland.

TRAPPED IN THE GHETTO

Ghettos were a stage in the Final Solution. They kept all the Jewish people prisoner in one place in the cities. Ghettos were surrounded by high walls and armed guards. They were very overcrowded. The Warsaw ghetto in Poland held 400,000 Jews in an area 2 per cent the size of the city.

Question Time

1. **a** What do Sources 1 and 2 tell us about how Jewish people felt all the time?
   b What do they tell us about how Jewish people managed to survive the conditions they lived in?
   Copy and complete this chart to show what you can find out.

	The Final Solution	How Jewish people felt	Living conditions
Source 1			
Source 2			
Source 3			

2. What questions would you like to ask about the sources?

3. What had the Jewish people in Source 1 done to be held at gun point?

SOURCE 3

The first step for the final aim (another code word, like solution) is the concentration of the Jews from the countryside into the large cities.

Reinhard Heydrich was a leading Nazi. Here he talks to his special duty groups about how to put the Final Solution into action.

There were many raids and arrests. Jews would be rounded up and shot, or sent to the concentration camps. Jews often died of disease or starvation in the ghettos. Food rations were kept tiny on purpose to starve some Jews to death. Some Jewish people were also worked to death.

SOURCE 5

The most horrible sight is of freezing children. Little children with bare feet, bare knees and torn clothes. Tonight I heard a child of three crying. The child will probably be found frozen to death tomorrow morning.

An extract from a book about living in the Warsaw ghetto, from a Jewish writer who was held there.

SOURCE 4

There are about 27,000 flats with an average of two and a half rooms each. They hold an average of 15.1 people per flat and six to seven people per room.

The SS officer in charge of the Warsaw ghetto reported these details about living conditions there.

SOURCE 6

A street used by Germans ran through the Lodz ghetto in Poland. A bridge was built and guarded so that Jews were kept separate.

SOURCE 7

Some ghettos were surrounded by fences, barbed wire or walls. In Warsaw the Jews had to pay a German firm to build the wall around the ghetto. In Cracow, Poland, the ghetto wall was made from gravestones taken from the Jewish cemetery.

A modern historian describes the ghettos.

TRYING TO STAY ALIVE

Jews in ghettos grouped together to try to stay alive. It was very hard but they did several things to stop themselves from going mad.

- They held secret lessons, meetings, lectures and prayer meetings.
- A secret newspaper was made.
- Some Jews worked as messengers, travelling to different ghettos to pass on information. It was dangerous work.
- Children were often smugglers, escaping to find food.

Activity Time

You have been asked to prepare a talk for a history conference on 'The ghettos in the Second World War'. Your talk will need to be over 300 words. Mention these important points.

- How and where the ghettos were set up.
- Why the ghettos were set up.
- How the Jewish people were treated in the ghettos.

HOW WAS THE FINAL SOLUTION PUT INTO PLACE?

One of the most famous images of the Holocaust is the front view of Auschwitz camp (see Source 1, page 156). A railway track ran right up to the front gate to bring in carriages full of Jews. The picture became a symbol of what was to be the future for millions of Jews in concentration and extermination camps. It is a symbol of the unknown, of fear and of death. Details of the extermination camps show us how horrendous the Holocaust really was. There are some difficult facts to face.

From the start of the war, groups of people were taken to forests. They were shot and piled into mass graves.

The Final Solution made the killing more organised, like a big industry. Even though Germany was being beaten in the USSR and Africa, killing Jews was still the Nazi Party's main priority.

WHO WAS THE ENEMY?

About six million Jews died during the Holocaust. But it wasn't just the Jews who were the target for Nazi violence and murder.

- The Germans killed non-Jewish people and prisoners of war in the countries they invaded.
- Nazis targeted handicapped people, homosexuals, Catholics, communists and gypsies.
- Teachers, writers and people who protected a Jewish person were also in trouble and were called political offenders.
- Anyone thought to be an enemy of the Nazi Party could be shot, beaten to death or taken to a camp.

It was the Jewish people who were the victims of **genocide**.

What does it mean?

Genocide
The killing of a race of people.

SOURCE 1

The entrance to Auschwitz camp.

WERE ALL THE CAMPS DEATH CAMPS?

In the plans for the Final Solution, six camps were set up just to murder Jews. These were all based in Poland, away from Germany so as not to be noticed.

Over 20 other camps were set up as work camps. In these, Jews and non-Jews were starved, tortured and killed. Possibly the most well-known was Auschwitz concentration camp (see Source 1).

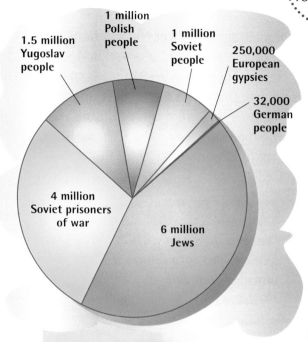

1.5 million Yugoslav people

1 million Polish people

1 million Soviet people

250,000 European gypsies

32,000 German people

4 million Soviet prisoners of war

6 million Jews

Estimates of the victims of Nazi occupation.

Activity Time

❶ Draw a large spider diagram as a class or in groups. The key words should all be about the Final Solution.
• Include ideas even if you are not sure they are true.
• Include anything you know about who, where, why and what happened in the Holocaust.

❷ Make a list of the questions that you would like to ask about the Final Solution. Include questions even if you think the answers are obvious.

Question Time

❶ Are these statements true or false?
a All concentration camps were extermination camps.
b Only Jews were killed in the extermination camps.
c All the Jews were killed using gas.
Explain your answers.

FROM THE GHETTOS TO THE CONCENTRATION CAMPS

In the ghettos, Jews themselves were given the job of choosing people to send to the concentration camps. Their goods were taken away and sold to pay for their transport. So some Jews paid for and organised many parts of the Holocaust. They had little choice, and many would try to save a few people if they could.

Jews in some ghettos tried to fight back. At the Warsaw ghetto, Jews fought against the SS (the Nazi security squad) for several weeks. But then the ghetto was burnt down. Once Jews were taken from the ghettos they were herded on to railroad cattle wagons, often with no food or drink.

SOURCE 2

We were taken to a train station, put into groups and crowded into railway carriages. We were each given a bucket as a toilet. We wondered where we were going. Hours passed. The smell became unbearable. The lice spread to all of us. Weak people began to die.

When Greece was invaded by Germany, Errikos Sevillias, a Jew, was sent to Auschwitz.

SOURCE 3

A carriage on a train carrying Jews to the camps.

ARRIVAL AND SELECTION

Old women, mothers with small children, pregnant women, and children under ten were usually taken to be executed straight away. Young boys would lie about their age and invent a craft so that they would be given work and stay alive.

SOURCE 4

The SS quickly split up the men and the women. They took the old and the sick and put them in a special line. The doctor who checked me tattooed my arm with the number 182699. My whole body was shaved. Then I was given a shower and some clothes that had huge red painted marks on them. This was so I could be easily spotted if I tried to escape.

Errikos Sevillias describes arriving at Auschwitz.

DAY BY DAY

Prisoners were given different jobs to do. But conditions were dreadful. Those who worked in the kitchens had a better chance of survival, because they could steal scraps of food. Possibly the worst job was taking the bodies from the gas chambers to the crematoria (where bodies are burnt).

The Nazis did not care about starving the prisoners to death. Disease spread quickly. In many camps some Jews were used in cruel medical experiments, mostly without anaesthetic. Doctors were testing to find the perfect Aryan person – for example, by injecting blue dye into brown eyes.

THE FINAL SOLUTION

- Prisoners not worked, starved or beaten to death faced death in the gas chambers.
- Carbon monoxide and Zyclon B gases were used to kill thousands of people.
- At Treblinka and Belzec extermination camps 140,000 people were killed each month by August 1942.
- Most gas chambers were fitted out as showers so that the prisoners would not panic.
- Bodies were burnt in ovens or left in mass pits.

MAXIMUM EFFICIENCY

What happened to the belongings of the prisoners and their bodies shows how the Nazi soldiers treated the Final Solution as a military operation. They had no thought for human life.

- Gold fillings from teeth were taken from bodies and melted down to send back to Germany.
- Hair that had been cut was used to make mattresses.

The Germans did not want evidence to be found. They had to get rid of all proof. People living near the sites of camps in Poland today can still see ash in the ground.

SOURCE 5

Most new arrivals did not know what was going to happen to them. They were asked to undress 'for the showers'. Sometimes they were handed soap and towels, and were promised hot coffee after their showers.

The gas chambers were made to look like shower rooms, with pipes, dressing rooms, clothes hooks and so on. If prisoners showed any signs of knowing what would happen to them, the guards would shout and kick them, set dogs on them or shoot them.

The Jews who went through this were often confused and weak after days of travelling in dark railway carriages.

Primo Levi, an Italian Jew, describes why most prisoners did not try to escape from the gas chambers.

ESCAPE

There was little chance of escape. Camps were guarded and surrounded by electric fencing and spotlights. Anyone who did try to escape was tortured, then shot or hanged in public. This was a strong message to the other prisoners. In 1943, 150 prisoners escaped from Treblinka camp and 300 from Sobibor camp. At Auschwitz there was a failed attempt to escape.

The glasses of victims at Auschwitz.

Question Time

❶ Why didn't prisoners try to escape more often?

❷ Look again at your spider diagram from page 157.
a How many of the points have turned out to be true?
b Find any that are wrong or too general and change them.

PEOPLE OF THE HOLOCAUST

Some people's stories of the Holocaust are more well known than others. Oscar Schindler, Martin Niemöller and Anne Frank are just three examples you may have heard of.

Oscar Schindler

Schindler was a wealthy Czechoslovakian factory owner. He joined the Nazi Party and was a Nazi spy. He had contacts high up in the party. He set up a factory near a ghetto and used 1200 Jewish people as cheap workers.

Activity Time

❶ In pairs find out more about the Final Solution. Collect ideas on a large sheet of paper. You can make these idea into a spider diagram or a list of bullet points. Your teacher might give you one of these topics to focus on.
• Work in the camps.   • Diet and living conditions.
• Rules and punishments. • Men, women and children.
• Proof that the Nazi soldiers treated the Jews as anima

❷ Explain to the rest of the class what you have found out
• Include one picture and a summary of five main point
• Try to use at least five new key words or examples.
• Explain what your picture shows and why you think it sums up your topic.

- Schindler began to protect his Jewish workers by bribing Nazi officials and forging documents. He stopped some Jews from being sent to concentration or extermination camps.
- Schindler's factory made bullets for the German army. All the bullets made were deliberately damaged and so were never used.
- Schindler was arrested several times, but he was always released.
- He had a reputation for liking women and alcohol.
- He was made famous in 1993 by the film *Schindler's List*.
- Jewish groups remember him as someone who risked his own life to save Jews.

Pastor Martin Niemöller

Niemöller was a minister in the Protestant church. He had a Jewish background. He spoke out against Nazi treatment of the churches. In 1936 he sent Hitler a letter of complaint. He was arrested and sent to a concentration camp. He was set free in 1945 at the end of the war.

Question Time

❶ Why was it important that the bullets made in Schindler's factory were never used?

❸ Look up Martin Niemöller on the Internet or in your library. Try to find the poem he wrote that became famous. Discuss the message of the poem with a partner.

SOURCE 7

A scene from the film *Schindler's List*. The characters here are Oscar Schindler (centre), his wife, and his factory manager, Itzhak Stern.

ANNE FRANK'S DIARY

You have possibly heard the name of this person before. Anne Frank was Jewish. She became famous because she wrote a diary before she was caught by the German army. She started her diary when she and her family went into hiding in Amsterdam, Holland. Her diary describes what it was like in hiding, and what she saw happening in Holland when it was taken over by Germany.

WHAT WAS HAPPENING TO JEWS IN AMSTERDAM?

After the German armies invaded Holland in 1940, anti-Jewish laws were brought in. Jewish companies had to register with the Nazi authorities so that they could be identified. Jews had to wear a yellow Star of David. They could only buy things at certain shops. They could only be outside until certain times.

Some Jewish businessmen stopped going to work so that they would not have to register. They knew that they would be taken to work camps in Germany. In 1941, German police began arresting all the Jews in Holland.

SOURCE 1

The Frank family in Amsterdam, 1941 – Margot (Anne's sister), Otto (her father), Anne and Edith (her mother).

Anne Frank's timeline

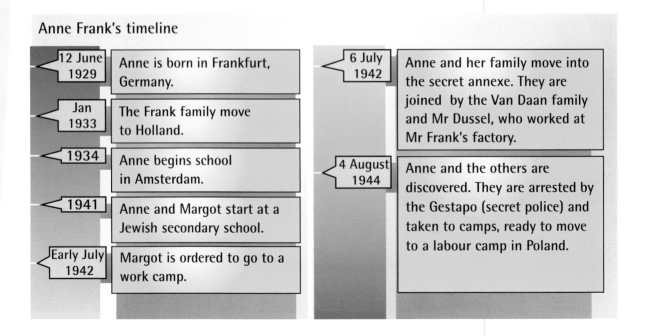

12 June 1929 — Anne is born in Frankfurt, Germany.

Jan 1933 — The Frank family move to Holland.

1934 — Anne begins school in Amsterdam.

1941 — Anne and Margot start at a Jewish secondary school.

Early July 1942 — Margot is ordered to go to a work camp.

6 July 1942 — Anne and her family move into the secret annexe. They are joined by the Van Daan family and Mr Dussel, who worked at Mr Frank's factory.

4 August 1944 — Anne and the others are discovered. They are arrested by the Gestapo (secret police) and taken to camps, ready to move to a labour camp in Poland.

THE SECRET ANNEXE

Otto Frank had decided that hiding was the only chance for his family to survive. He prepared some attic rooms hidden behind his office. This was the secret annexe. He had moved in some furniture and some basic belongings.

When Margot was called to report to the Nazi authorities, he had to bring his plans forward. The family had to move at once from their home. They wore several layers of clothes and carried all they could in two bags each. They had to be careful, because they did not want to be noticed by the police.

A plan of the secret annexe, the name Anne's family gave to their hiding place.

SOURCE 2

We have to whisper and tread lightly during the day. Otherwise the people in the warehouse might hear us.

An entry from Anne's diary for 11 July 1942.

SOURCE 3

Normal people don't know what books mean to us, shut up in here. Reading, learning and the radio are our only fun.

Anne's diary entry for 11 July 1943.

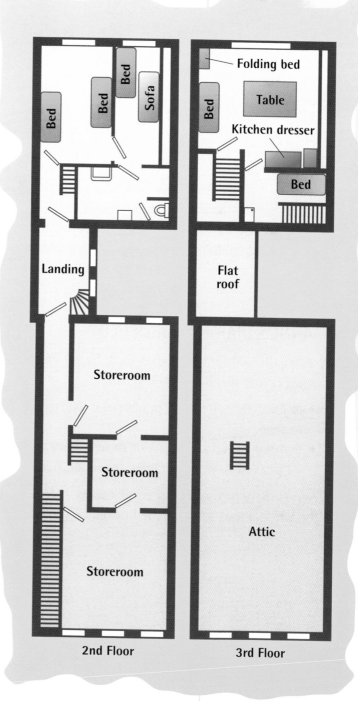

2nd Floor

3rd Floor

SOURCE 4

Our Jewish friends are being taken away. It is impossible to escape. Most of the people in the camp (in Holland) have their heads shaved. If it is as bad as this in Holland, whatever will it be like where they are sent to abroad? The British radio speaks of people being gassed.

Anne Frank's diary entry for 9 October 1942.

SOURCE 5

Evening after evening the grey and green army lorries go past. The Germans ring at every door to ask if there are any Jews living in the house. If there are, then the whole family has to go at once. No one has a chance unless they go into hiding.

Anne Frank's diary entry for 19 November 1942.

DEAR KITTY

Anne writes each diary entry to 'Kitty' as if she were a close friend. Anne's diary tells us about what it was like to be a Jewish teenager during the war. Anne describes her fears, moods and day-to-day life. She moans and jokes about other people in the annexe. She writes about her parents. She writes about her feelings for her close friend Peter van Daan. Anne decided that after the war she would publish her diary.

ANNE'S DIARY IS PUBLISHED

After the war, Anne's diaries were found in the annexe and given to her father.

- In 1947 he edited and published a shortened diary, for teenagers to read.
- In 1989 a second version of Anne's dairy was published, showing all sides of Anne's character, including her inner thoughts.

Anne's diary has sold millions of copies. It teaches people all over the world about some of the horrors of the Holocaust.

Question Time

❶ What rights were taken away from Anne and her family before they went into hiding? Look back to page 162 for a reminder.

❷ a Make a list of the sorts of things that Anne could do when she was in hiding.
b Make a list of the sorts of things she could *not* do.

SOURCE 6

Everyone thinks I'm showing off when I talk, that I'm ridiculous when I don't talk, rude when I answer, lazy when I'm tired, selfish when I eat one bite more than I should, etc., etc. All day long I hear what a frustrating child I am and although I pretend not to mind, I do.

Anne's diary entry for 30 January 1943.

Question Time

1 Why do you think that writing a diary was so important to Anne?

2 Unlike many Jewish families, the Frank family survived for two years in hiding before being arrested. What helped them to survive?

SUPPORT NETWORK

Anne and her family and friends could not survive in hiding without food and help from the outside. Five of Mr Frank's workers agreed to help them.

- Forged ration cards were made by the Resistance in Holland (the secret group working against the Nazis). The cards got them food without too much suspicion.
- Miep Gies, her husband Jan, Mr Kraler, Mr Koophuis and Elli Vossen helped the hideaways for the two years until they were discovered.

THE END OF THE STORY

The secret annexe was discovered on 4 August 1944. Everyone was arrested and sent to Auschwitz extermination camp in Poland. Mrs Frank died of starvation in Auschwitz. Mr Van Daan was gassed to death there. Mr Dussel died at Neuengamme camp, near Hamburg. Peter Van Daan died in Mauthausen camp in Austria. Anne, her sister Margot and Mrs Van Daan were moved to Bergen Belsen camp, and died there. Anne and Margot died from catching typhus. A month after their death the camp was set free by the Allies. Mr Frank survived the Holocaust.

SOURCE 7

Anne Frank's name is on the last list of people taken from Westerbork transportation camp to Auschwitz camp in 1944.

JUDENTRANSPORT AUS DEN NIEDERLANDEN - LAGER WESTERBORK			
Haeftlinge			
301.✓Engers	Isidor — ✓30.4. 93 -	Kaufmann	
302✓ Engers	Leonard 15.6. 20 -	Lamdarbeiter	
303✓ Franco	Manfred - ✓1.5. 05 —	Verleger	
304. Frank	Arthur 22.8. 81	Kaufmann	
305. Frank ✗	Isaac ✓29.11.87	Installateur	
306. Frank	Margot 16.2. 26	ohne	
307. Frank ✓	Otto ✓12.5. 89	Kaufmann	
308.✓ Frank-Hollaender	Edith 16.1. 00	ohne	
309. Frank	Anneliese 12.6. 29	ohne	
310. v.Franck	Sara — 27.4. 02-	Typistin	
311. Franken	Rozanna 16.5. 96-	Landarbeiter	
312.✓ Franken-Weyand	Johanna 24.12.96✓	Landbauer	
313. Franken	Hermann —✓12.5.74	ohne	

WHAT HAPPENED WHEN PEOPLE FOUND OUT ABOUT THE HOLOCAUST?

SOURCE 1

Here are the facts about Belsen. Within its barbed wire fences, covering about fifteen acres, there are 40,000 men, women and children. They are German, Polish, Russian and six other nationalities.

Of the total, 4250 are badly ill or dying. I doubt if they can be saved. 25,600, mainly women, are ill or actually dying from starvation.

SOURCE 2

This is something that we can hardly believe. I can quote the young tommy (British) gunner, who was on duty. He said, 'Now I believe every word I've heard about the Nazis.'

SOURCE 3

This day was the most horrible of my life. You will be glad to know that we have caught alive the commander of the camp, Kramer, and his SS guards. They are being made to carry the bodies. I have never seen British soldiers so angry as the men who opened Belsen camp.

Richard Dimbleby, who worked for the BBC, was the first reporter to see the Belsen concentration camp in Germany when it was set free at the end of the war. Belsen was a prison camp rather than an extermination camp. But it was still badly overcrowded. Dimbleby broke down in tears during the recording of what he saw. Sources 1–3 are extracts from his report.

Question Time

❶ Study Sources 1 to 3. What words can be used to describe Richard Dimbleby's feelings when he saw the Belsen concentration camp?

❷ a Does Dimbleby show us what he thinks of the Nazis?
b Discuss this question with a partner.

❸ Why do you think that SS guards were made to carry dead bodies?

DID THE WORLD KNOW ABOUT THE HOLOCAUST BEFORE 1945?

- Although the Nazis wanted to keep the Final Solution a secret, a news report came from Poland to the Allies and to the Pope as early as 1942.
- British and American governments allowed just a few refugees into their countries.
- America and Britain would not bomb the camps, because they thought there was not enough proof. Nazi reports wrote in code and spoke of 'resettling' the Jews and giving them 'special treatment'.
- Christian churches also did little. The Pope gave his sympathy and asked for people to be treated fairly. Religious leaders in western Europe criticised the Holocaust. Ministers in Germany did not.

SOURCE 4

So far three million have died. It is the biggest mass killing in history, and it goes on daily, hourly. I have been talking to Allied troops for three years now and they are always the same. They don't believe it.

Arthur Koestler, an American journalist, writing in the *New York Times* in January 1944.

SOURCE 5

If we hadn't seen those ghastly skeletons and great heaps of bodies, I don't think we would have believed it. Even now it doesn't seem possible that humans could sink so low.

George MacDonald Fraser saw newsreel footage of Belsen in a cinema. Fraser survived the war in Burma. He was a reporter and a writer.

Question Time

1 What do Sources 4 and 5 tell us about what people thought about the Holocaust?

2 Read Source 5. Why do you think that newsreel films of camps like Belsen were shown in cinemas at the end of the war?

HOW DID PEOPLE REACT?

Many SS officers left the camps when Germany was close to losing the war. Local people who had worked in the camps also left and hid in their villages. When Russian and British troops got to the camps they faced solid proof of the mass killings.

- Some Nazis were caught alive and arrested.
- Local people were made to walk through camps to see what had been happening under their noses.
- Thousands of bodies were buried as quickly as possible to stop more disease from spreading.

SOURCE 6

Female SS guards at Bergen-Belsen camp in Germany. They were made to bury the bodies of those people they had helped to kill.

Question Time

❶ Study Source 6. Why are the SS guards burying the bodies instead of the Allied soldiers?

❷ Why do you think that Allied soldiers made local people walk through the camps?

THE NEED FOR JUSTICE

Justice is fair treatment. The Allies wanted to catch the leaders of the Holocaust and see justice carried out. In 1945 a war crimes court was set up in Nuremberg. It put 22 Holocaust leaders on trial. Hitler, Himmler and Göebbels escaped trial. They had all committed suicide at the end of the war in Europe.

THE NUREMBERG TRIALS – VERDICT IN 1946

- The trial was organised by the USA, Britain, France and the USSR.
- The new charge of 'crimes against humanity' was brought in to deal with the Holocaust.
- Nineteen men were found guilty.
- Twelve men were hanged. Three were given life sentences. Four were given shorter prison sentences.
- There were many eye-witnesses and huge amounts of detailed evidence of the Final Solution. The Nazis had been very organised. Their detailed records helped to prove their guilt.

SOURCE 7

Hans Heinrich Lammers, Hitler's right-hand man, on trial in Nuremberg in 1947.

SIMILAR TRIALS

Other trials took place all over Europe. In the 20 years after the Holocaust, over 20,000 people were taken to court for war crimes. Trials for war criminals from the Second World War still take place today.

DIFFICULT QUESTIONS

As well as the problem of war criminals, countries and people have had to come to terms with the Holocaust. Many different groups of people helped or ignored the Final Solution. Many people felt guilty for their own actions or that of their parents or their country.

SOURCE 8

These wrongs have been so planned, so evil and so devastating, that the world cannot ignore them because it cannot survive them being repeated.

This was said by Justice of the Supreme Court Robert Jackson. He represented the USA at the Nuremberg Trials.

SOURCE 9

Most of those accused of murder did not realise the seriousness of their crimes. For example, one man did not feel too guilty as he had only killed 5000 people. He said, 'Why am I being punished? It was only 5000. Ohlendorf killed 20,000. That's something completely different.'

A commander of Soviet volunteers in the German army said this in an interview in 1989–90.

Activity Time

Here are some difficult questions. Discuss them in groups.

❶ Are owners of factories producing Zyclon B guilty of mass murder?

❷ Are the camp guards as guilty as the commandants?

❸ The Allies knew of the mass murder well before the end of the war. Should they take some blame?

❹ Should survivors who had belongings taken away get compensation?

❺ Should the people of Germany pay for their country's mistakes?

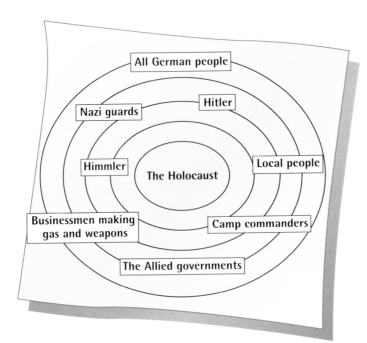

Who is guilty? Who is to blame? Do you agree that the people closest to the centre of the ripple should take most responsibility for the Holocaust?

Question Time

1 'All that is needed is for good men to stand still.'
a What does this quote suggest about the blame for the Holocaust?
b Do you agree?
c Discuss this idea in a group.

2 Who do you think should take most responsibility for the Holocaust?
a Decide on the amount of blame each of these groups should have:

- factory owners who produced Zyclon B
- camp guards
- commandants
- Nazi SS guards
- the Allies.

b Draw them in a triangle. Put the most guilty at the top of the triangle.
c Compare triangles with your partner. Discuss any differences.

WHAT HAPPENED TO SURVIVORS?

The survivors of the Holocaust had many problems to deal with. Many ex-prisoners actually became more ill after they had been freed. They seemed to stop fighting for survival. Millions of people were homeless and without any family or friends to help them.

Displaced Persons (DPs)

Displaced Persons are people who lost their homes during the war. There were about 30 million DPs in total, including many prisoners of war and labourers.

Taking action

- Jewish organisations helped to trace relatives and reunite families.
- The Red Cross and the Allied armies opened shelters for the DPs.
- Survivors needed to work to earn a living, so most missed out on an education or training.

Activity Time

Match up these sentences to show whether they are arguments for or against taking Nazi war criminals to court. Discuss your answers in pairs.

Your teacher may then put you in a group to argue for or against war crimes trials to the rest of the class.
a Trials cost thousands of pounds, which could be spent in better ways.
b Families of the victims need to get justice.
c Cruel people in the world today need to know that they cannot get away with such crimes.
d Most of the accused criminals are very old and ill.
e Many of the accused criminals were only following orders and would have been shot if they did not do their job.

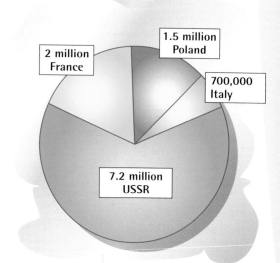

Approximate figures for Displaced Persons.

2 million France

1.5 million Poland

700,000 Italy

7.2 million USSR

Creating a Jewish homeland in Israel was a step towards healing after the Holocaust for some Jews. When Palestine was split up to make Israel in 1948, many Arabs were forced to move. This has caused arguments and wars over land ever since.

Activity Time

Copy a large version of this ripple diagram to build up a pattern of how the lives of survivors were affected.

Here are statements of different effects on Holocaust survivors. Put each statement on a card and place it on your ripple diagram to show how directly people were affected. Alternatively you could write your statements on your diagram in pencil. Remember that the worst effect will be at the centre of your diagram.

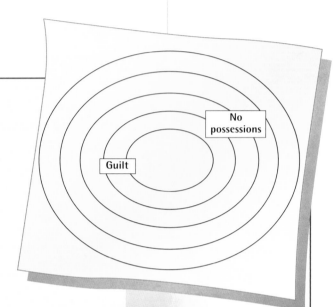

How did the Holocaust affect people's lives?

Survivors had no belongings or homes.

Survivors felt guilty that they had lived.

Families and friends had been lost or split up.

Memories of the Holocaust stayed in their minds.

Some Jews were still treated badly. In Poland locals killed a thousand Jews when they returned 'home'.

Some Jews lost faith in God and/or man.

Survivors could not grieve properly. They had no graves to visit and no information about how their friends or family died.

Homes had been ruined or taken over by other people.

Some survivors wanted revenge or justice, and for others to never forget the Holocaust.

Health problems, caused by malnutrition, continued.

EXPRESSIONS OF THE HOLOCAUST

Never Shall I Forget

Never shall I forget that night
The first night in the camp
Which has turned my life into one long night,
Seven times cursed and seven times sealed.

Never shall I forget that smoke.
Never shall I forget the little faces of the
  children
Whose bodies I saw turned into **wreaths** of
  smoke
Beneath a silent blue sky.

Never shall I forget those flames
Which **consumed** my faith for ever.
Never shall I forget the **nocturnal** silence
Which deprived me for all **eternity** of the desire
  to live.

Never shall I forget those moments
Which murdered my God and my soul
And turned my dreams into dust.

Never shall I forget these things,
Even if I am condemned to live
as long as God himself.

Never.

Elie Wiesel (born 1928)

Elie Wiesel was a Romanian Jew who was sent
to Auschwitz and Buchenwald labour camps.
His mother, father and sister died in the
Holocaust. He is a Professor in America. In
1986 he won the Nobel Prize for Peace.

The Trains

Signed by Franz Paul Stangl, Commandant,
There is in Berlin a document,
An order of **transmittal** from Treblinka

248 **freight** cars of clothing,
400,000 gold watches,
25 freight cars of women's hair.

Some fine clothing was kept, some was
  pulped for paper.
The finest watches were never melted down.
All the women's hair was used for mattresses,
  or dolls.

Would these words like to use some of that
  same paper?
One of those watches may pulse in your own
  wrist.
Does someone you know collect dolls, or
sleep on human hair?

He is dead at last, Commandant Stangl of
  Treblinka,
But the camp's three **syllables** still sound like
  freight cars
Straining around a curve, Treblinka

Treblinka. Clothing, time in gold watches,
Women's hair for mattresses and dolls' heads.
Treblinka. The trains from Treblinka.

William Heyen (born 1940)

What does it mean?

Wreaths – Flowers of respect for a grave.
Consumed – Eaten up.
Nocturnal – At night.
Eternity – For all time.
Transmittal – Passing on or moving.
Freight – Goods.
Syllables – Parts of a word that are
sounded.

Question Time

❶ Why do you think that Elie Wiesel repeats
one phrase several times in *Never Shall I
Forget*?

❷ How do you feel when you read about hair,
gold, clothing and watches in *The Trains*?

❸ Does it matter to historians that William
Heyen had not been part of the Holocaust?

❹ Which poem do you like the most
and why?

EXPLORING THE HOLOCAUST – WHAT QUESTIONS AND ISSUES REMAIN?

The word 'Holocaust' came to be used for the deliberate murder of a whole race. It is an event that is difficult to understand.

Activity Time

1 Here are some key questions that we have not answered.

a Why didn't more Jews fight back?

b How did the Jews rebel in the Warsaw ghetto?

c What sort of people tried to help the Jews?

d Could Britain and the USA have done more?

e Why did the German people let it happen?

f Why didn't the Christian churches do more?

Work in a group to find out more about one of the big questions **a–f**. Your teacher might suggest which question to cover and where you can find information. Write your big question in the middle of a large piece of paper. Start by writing what you think some of the answers might be in pencil. Change them later if you were wrong.

2 In groups, present your findings to the rest of the class. Use at least two of these methods:

• role play
• pictures
• summary speeches
• display of key points
• factfile
• bibliography
• video
• documentary
• a mini lesson.

All groups should give the rest of the class the chance to ask questions. But don't worry if you do not have a final answer.

SO, HOW AND WHY DID THE HOLOCAUST HAPPEN?

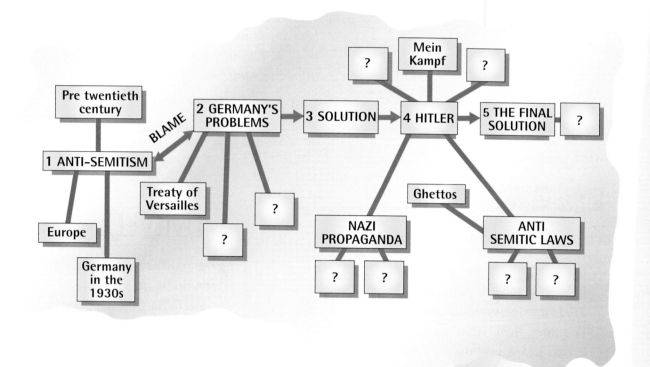

Copy and fill in this ideas diagram to help you to answer the big question 'How and why did the Holocaust happen?' Some of the key points are already included. But add some more using points, names and examples.

How and why did the Holocaust happen?

Use the ideas diagram as a plan for a report to answer the big question. The numbered sections could become separate paragraphs. You will need to add the following.

- An introduction – say what the Holocaust was and what you are going to argue about.
- Main body – paragraphs 1–5.
- A conclusion – what do you think is the best answer we can get?

THE LESSONS OF THE HOLOCAUST

In 1999 Anthony Sawoniuk, aged 78, was put on trial in Britain and sentenced to life imprisonment for murdering 18 Jewish people during the Second World War. His trial caused a lot of debate in Britain. People used all the arguments that you have seen on page 171. War crimes trials like this one remind people of events in history like the Holocaust. Mass killings and genocide have taken place in more recent years. This suggests there are lessons still to be learned.

SOURCE 1

The trial (of Sawoniuk) is a symbolic beacon. It reminds us of the cruelty of the past. It reminds us of all the danger of allowing racist dictators to rule.

Lord Janner QC, commenting on the case.

SOURCE 2

The world has been shocked by the killings in Kosovo, where maybe 5000 Albanians died in just a few months. At Srebrenica more than 7000 were murdered in just a few days in July 1995. Most of these people had been shot in the head. They were then dumped in mass graves. The western countries should take some responsibility, because they refused to help.

This article was in the *Independent* newspaper in November 1999. It refers to the extermination of a large number of Muslim men in Srebrenica. The United Nations took no action to prevent the shootings.

Activity Time

❶ Do you think that criminals should be put on trial for something that happened more than 50 years ago?

❷ Write an evaluation of this unit answering these main questions.
a What did you know about the Holocaust before this unit?
b What shocked or surprised you the most?
c What do you think you will remember the most?
d What three big lessons have you learned?

❸ As a class, discuss what you think are the most important lessons to be learned from studying the Holocaust.

Unit 20: Twentieth-century medicine – how has it changed the lives of ordinary people?

BETTER HEALTH – LONGER LIFE: WHY?

It's true that medicine has changed the lives of millions of people. But it hasn't changed things for everyone. And not every medical discovery has been for the better. This unit will tell you more about twentieth-century medicine.

Drains and sewers

Vaccinating babies

Check-ups by school nurse

Good diet

Straightening crooked teeth

Taking out burst appendix

Clean water

Antibiotic drugs

Toilets

Spectacles

Setting a broken wrist

Taking out infected tonsils

WHAT KEEPS US HEALTHY?

Everything in the bubbles on this page keeps us healthy. Read these bubbles carefully. Then think about all the other things that keep us fit and healthy. Some of them will be connected with:

- medicines and drugs
- operations
- living conditions (public health)
- preventing disease in the first place.

Sort your list under the headings on the table. Then fill in the gaps.

Medicine	Surgery	Public health	Preventative medicine
Antibiotic drugs	Taking out infected tonsils	Toilets	Flu jabs
	Fitting grommets in 'glue' ears	Clean water	**Vaccinating** babies
			Good diet

Activity Time

TWO FAMILIES – ONE HUNDRED YEARS APART

In 1900, the Dawson family lived in
Whitefield, near Manchester

John Dawson	Aged 37	Grocer at the local Co-op
Alice Dawson	Aged 35	Part-time telephonist at the local telephone exchange
Harry Dawson	Aged 16	Apprenticed at a local electrical engineering company
Kathleen Dawson	Aged 14	Shop assistant in a department store in Manchester
Jack Dawson	Aged 13	Errand boy in the local bank
Ann Dawson	Aged 10	At school
Ellis Dawson	Aged 6	At school

The daughter has TB (tuberculosis – a disease that can kill). The doctor says she should go to a health clinic in Switzerland where the air is cleaner.

The daughter has fallen off her bike. The ambulance has taken her to the nearest hospital. An X-ray shows she has badly hurt her back. She is taken to a special spinal unit.

The local council want to dig up the road and lay a sewer. This is so every house in the road can have a toilet that flushes.

The father has had a heart attack. He needs open heart surgery. But the waiting list is very long. It could take many months.

What does it mean?

Vaccination
Injection against diseases like smallpox and polio. The injection introduces a small sample of disease to the body, which the body learns how to fight. This stops the disease returning.

Antibiotic
A drug, like penicillin. It is produced by living things that can destroy or stop the growth of harmful bacteria and disease.

In 2000, the Freeman family lived in Norwich, Norfolk.

Michael Freeman	Aged 37	Manager in the local supermarket
Jennifer Freeman	Aged 35	Part-time teacher in the local comprehensive school
Daniel Freeman	Aged 13	At school
Rachel Freeman	Aged 10	At school

The father has been knocked down by a runaway horse. He has damaged his leg. Workmen take him home on a stretcher they have made. His wife sends for the doctor.

The mother discovers she is going to have another baby. She is worried that the family cannot afford another mouth to feed.

The mother has kidney failure. She is having complicated treatment every week while she waits for a transplant operation.

The son has diphtheria. (a dangerous infection of the throat that could stop someone breathing). The doctor wants him to have a new anti-poison drug that could cure him.

Not all of these events happened to each family all at once, or even at all. But they are things that could have happened. Each thing would have presented problems to the family.

1 Illnesses and accidents can happen to any family at almost any time.

Working with a partner, match the events in the bubbles to the people in the Dawson and Freeman families.

2 Explain why you made the decisions you did. Remember to think about medicine, and what could or could not be done at the time.

3 Make a wall poster showing what is happening to each family. Remember to focus on medicine.

FREE AT THE POINT OF DELIVERY?

The Dawson family in 1900 and the Freeman family in 2000 had very different experiences of medical help. Just how did people at the beginning of the twentieth century get their health care?

WHAT WAS THE SITUATION IN 1900?

People had to pay if they wanted to see a doctor. This was difficult for poor families. Some poor families saved a few pence each week with a 'friendly society'. This meant they had money for medical help if they needed it. Some doctors started a savings 'club' for their own patients.

Most large towns, like Cardiff, Newcastle and Manchester, had their own hospitals. These were called infirmaries. In country areas, doctors joined together to run cottage hospitals. There was almost no **preventative care**.

The government had a big shock in 1899. Young men were called up to join the army to fight in the Boer War. When army doctors examined these men, they found that two out of every three were unfit to fight.

LIBERAL GOVERNMENT REFORMS 1906–14

In 1906, the Liberal government came to power. It brought in a lot of reforms that were aimed at helping poorer people lead healthier lives.

Copy the table below, which shows some of the reforms brought in by the Liberal government. Ask your teacher or use a reference book to find out about each one. Then, in the right hand column, explain how each reform helped people to lead healthier lives.

What does it mean?

Preventative care
Measures that stop people falling ill in the first place.

What?	When?	How did it help people lead healthier lives?
School Meals	1906	
School Medical Service	1907	
Children's Act	1908	
Old Age Pensions	1908	
Housing Act	1909	
National Insurance	1911	

THE BEVERIDGE REPORT 1942

In the middle of the Second World War, the British Government began looking ahead. It asked Sir William Beveridge to suggest ways in which it could help the sick, unemployed, low-paid workers and retired people. In 1942, Beveridge produced a report that recommended enormous reforms. He wanted the state to look after people **'from the cradle to the grave'**. He said he was waging war on the five giants of:

- Want
- Ignorance
- Disease.
- Squalor
- Idleness

We are going to look at how the war was waged on disease.

What does it mean?

'From the cradle to the grave'
From the time you are born to the time you die.

THE NATIONAL HEALTH SERVICE

After the Second World War, the new Labour government began to set up the National Health Service. The Minister for Health, Aneurin Bevan, said that the NHS should do the following things.

- Provide medical services for everyone.
- Be free for people to use whenever they needed help.

I want everyone to have free medical care whenever they need it?

Aneurin Bevan thought of the idea of the National Health Service. The NHS is the system that we use in the UK today.

Many doctors were against the NHS. They were afraid the government would tell them where to work, when to work, and how much they could earn. Aneurin Bevan worked out a system with them. Doctors were to be paid a set amount for each NHS patient, and were allowed to treat private, fee-paying patients if they wanted to.

Parliament had to agree to the government's proposals. MPs debated and agreed to the National Health Bill, and on 5 July 1948 the National Health Service began.

SETTING UP THE NATIONAL HEALTH SERVICE

SOURCE 1

This cartoon was published in the newspaper the *Daily Mirror*, in September 1945.

SOURCE 2

If the Bill is passed, no patient or doctor will feel safe from interference by some government rule or regulation.

From the *British Medical Journal*, 18 January 1946. This was the doctors' journal. It was linked to the British Medical Association, which spoke for the doctors.

SOURCE 3

Doctors are afraid of becoming government servants. They are afraid of losing their independence.

From a newspaper the *Daily Sketch*, 5 February 1946.

SOURCE 4

Medical treatment should be available to rich and poor people. They should be given whatever treatment they need, and this must be free. Worry about money stops people recovering quickly and may stop them asking for help in the first place. It is usually mothers who suffer most because they put the needs of their family before their own needs. No society can call itself civilised if sick people are denied medical help because they are poor. Rich and poor must be treated alike.

This is part of a speech made by Aneurin Bevan in 1946. It explains why he wants Parliament to agree to the National Health Bill.

SOURCE 5

This cartoon was published in the magazine *Punch* in 1948. It shows Aneurin Bevan giving the doctors unpleasant medicine.

DOTHEBOYS HALL
"It still tastes awful."

Question Time

1 Read Source 4. Why did Aneurin Bevan think that we needed to have a National Health Service?

2 Look at Sources 1 to 5.
a Why did some people think that we needed to have a National Health Service?
b Why were some people against setting up a National Health Service?

3 Look at Source 5. The person in the large hat is Aneurin Bevan. The other people are doctors. Look at the doctors' faces. What do you think the doctors think about the National Health Service?

4 Pretend you are a journalist who has been sent to interview Aneurin Bevan in the 1950s. What would you want to ask him about the problems and successes in setting up the NHS?

WHAT DID IT ALL COST?

The National Health Service was giving free health care to everyone. But no one knew how many people would need the free care. So no one knew how much the NHS would cost.

The government paid for the NHS from the **taxes** people paid. This worked well until there was an emergency. In order to pay for the Korean War (1950–3) the government made the taxes higher, and made people pay for every prescription form they took to the chemist. Aneurin Bevan resigned in protest.

IS THERE A DOWN-SIDE TO MODERN SURGERY AND MEDICINE?

Modern, high-tech medicine can keep people alive who would have died in earlier years. Modern drugs can control, and sometimes wipe out altogether, killer diseases like smallpox and diphtheria. Research laboratories are working to find drugs that will cure cancer and **AIDS**. All this is very, very expensive.

The development of modern surgery and medicine does have its problems. People may end up living longer, but sometimes the quality of their lives is very poor. They may, for example, have been saved from death after a horrific accident, but be brain-damaged.

Modern drugs can have very bad side effects that no one realised when the drugs were being produced.

All hospitals and doctors have to work within a budget. They cannot spend more money than the government gives them from the taxes that everyone pays.

What does it mean?

Taxes
This is money that goes to the government. People who earn money pay taxes. We pay taxes on things like alcohol, cigarettes and cars. The government spends this money on things that benefit everyone.

AIDS
A virus that can spread through the bloodstream. It stops you fighting off any other disease or illness you may get.

DIFFICULT DECISIONS

In every hospital in the country, hard choices have to be made. These are to do with:

- cost, because there is not enough money to do everything
- the quality of life a person would have after treatment
- the ending of life by switching off a life support machine.

Work through this next activity about 'difficult decisions'. Remember that there are no easy choices and no right answers.

Activity Time

Think about the people listed below. They all need heart surgery in the next few weeks so they can live normal lives. But there is a waiting list at the NHS hospitals.

- A 22-year-old single mother, who has two children.
- A boy who is four years old.
- An 80-year-old woman, who is an important key fund-raiser for an AIDS charity.
- A single man, aged 45, who is a skilled surgeon.
- A 17-year-old girl, who lives rough on the streets of London.
- A woman aged 40, who travels around dangerous parts of the world to report on the news.
- A man aged 65, who has worked hard all his life and is looking forward to his well-earned retirement.
- A 25-year-old man, who has multiple sclerosis (a wasting disease of the muscles).

❶ Put these people in order.
   a Who do you think should have the operation first?
   b Who should have the operation second?
   c Third? and so on.
   Work through the list until everyone has a place.

❷ Compare your order with what other people in your class have done. Talk about why some people have a different order from you.

THE NHS AFTER FIFTY YEARS

This is what is happening in the NHS 50 years after it was set up.

- Difficult decisions, like the ones you have been working on, are being made more and more often. This is because modern medicine gives people the chance of treatments that were not even dreamed of in the early days of the NHS.
- Most people are being charged directly for part of the cost of drugs and treatments. This is because of the expense of high-tech medicine.
- Some people have free NHS treatment. This is because they do not earn enough or have long-term illnesses.

The grid below compares 1948 with 2000.

1948	Cost?	2000	Cost?
Prescription	Free	Prescription	£6 per item
Eye test	Free	Eye test	£15.01 for a basic test
Glasses	Free	Glasses	From £35 for a child and £60 for an adult
Dental check-up	Free	Dental check-up	£4.76
A dental filling	Free	A dental filling	From £5.24
A set of false teeth	Free	A set of false teeth	From £100
A visit to or by the doctor	Free	A visit to or by the doctor	Free

What does it cost?
- 1950 (the first full year of the NHS) = £446 million
- 2000 (50 years on) = £49 billion (£49,000 million)

Some people choose to pay for private medical treatment rather than use the NHS. They do this so that they can get treatment quickly, choose a time that's best for them, and have comfortable, even luxurious, surroundings.

But even so, in the 1990s, 89 per cent of spending on health care in Britain was by the NHS.

Question Time

❶ Look at the chart above.
a Do you think it is fair to compare things in this way?
b Explain your answer.

❷ a Should the government keep on funding the NHS, no matter how much it costs?
b Explain your answer.

LOOKING FOR THE 'MAGIC BULLET'

In the early 1900s, scientists were looking for a wonder drug that would work inside people's bodies, killing disease. They called this unknown wonder drug a 'magic bullet'.

PAUL ERLICH

In 1909, Paul Erlich developed the first 'magic bullet'. This was called Salvarsan 606. It cured **syphilis**. But the drug was difficult to inject into people's veins and painful for the patient.

GERHARD DAMAGK

Gerhard Damagk was a scientist working on a red dye called prontosil. He discovered that it stopped the **streptococcus microbe** from multiplying in mice.

In 1932, Gerhard's daughter was dying from blood poisoning. So he injected her with a massive dose of prontosil. She recovered. Was this the second magic bullet?

SULPHONAMIDE

A team of French scientists discovered that the vital ingredient in prontosil that acted on germs was sulphonamide. Sulphonamide drugs were made to attack the microbes that caused tonsillitis, **pneumonia, puerperal fever** and scarlet fever.

But sulphonamide could damage a person's liver and kidneys. Also, it did not attack all diseases.

What is it?

Syphilis
A sexually transmitted disease.

Streptococcus
Microbes that cause various infections.

Microbes
A tiny living thing (organisms).

Pneumonia
Inflammation of the lungs when they fill with fluid.

Puerperal fever
A dangerous fever caused by childbirth.

PENICILLIN

The most important magic bullet was developed by three men:

- Alexander Fleming
- Howard Flory, and
- Ernst Chain.

Alexander Fleming discovered penicillin in 1928. It was developed by Howard Flory and Ernst Chain and put into mass production by the USA during the Second World War. It was used to fight:

- deep infection in war wounds.
- a wide range of infectious illnesses.

But some types of bacteria have become immune to penicillin. And some people who have been given penicillin many times find that it doesn't work on them any more. They have to be given stronger and stronger drugs to help them fight disease.

MORE HARM THAN GOOD?

- Drug companies develop hundreds of new drugs every year.
- Some drugs can be bought over the counter without the advice of a doctor.
- Not all companies have tested their products fully before selling them.
- Drug companies have to make profits for their shareholders.

THALIDOMIDE AND LARGACTIL

In 1961, a German company produced a drug called thalidomide. It helped pregnant women to stay well. But it hadn't been tested for its effects on their unborn babies. When these babies were born, they had terrible deformities. Some had tiny arms and legs. Others had no arms or legs at all.

In the 1980s, Largactil was used to calm mentally ill people. It was later discovered that the drug caused irreversible brain damage.

PROZAC

In the 1990s, people who were finding it difficult to cope with everyday life used Prozac. Many called it their 'happy pill'. But later it was found that it was addictive and could cause schizophrenia, depression and even suicide.

In 1964, the British Government set up the Committee on the Safety of Drugs to screen all newly developed drugs.

ALTERNATIVE AND COMPLEMENTARY MEDICINE

Some people prefer alternative, drug-free medicine. Others use different sorts of medicine side by side (complementary) with standard medical treatments.

Question Time

1 a Make a graph to show the good things (pluses) and bad things (minuses) of modern medicine.
b Are there more 'pluses' than 'minuses'? (Write down the number of each.)

2 Use your graph to answer this question: 'Have changes in medicine improved everything for everyone?'

Factfile

Acupuncture

People in ancient China believed that energy (called ch'i) flowed through their bodies. They became ill when this ch'i was blocked and couldn't flow freely. Thousands of people still believe this today. An acupuncturist finds the point at which a person's ch'i is blocked, and pushes a needle into the place. Sometimes a lot of needles are needed and they are pushed in to different depths and for different lengths of time. When the ch'i is freed, the person will get better.

Aromatherapy

People in ancient Egypt used aromatic oils like eucalyptus, lavender and cloves to cure skin problems. Today, aromatherapists massage oils into their clients skin. They say that all kinds of problems and conditions are helped in this way.

Chiropractic

Chiropractors believe that a person can only be healthy if their muscles, skeleton and nervous system are working together properly. They never use drugs. They treat their patients by manipulating their spine and other joints.

Herbal medicine

For thousands of years people have used seeds and fruit, flowers and bark, herbs and spices to treat all kinds of illnesses and conditions. Today, the most commonly treated illnesses are colds and 'flu, sleep problems and vomiting.

Homeopathy

Homeopathic doctors believe that the body has the power to heal itself. They have their own homeopathic remedies based on natural substances. They will use chemical drugs when necessary, but only in the smallest possible amounts.

Osteopathy

Osteopaths use all the usual medicines, but concentrate more on the links between a patient's internal organs, muscles and skeletons.

Reflexology

Reflexologists believe that energy flows through the body and ends in a person's feet. So by massaging a person's feet, their condition will be helped.

Question time

1 Why do you think that some people prefer not to use modern medical treatments?

2 Why do you think that some doctors don't like alternative sorts of medicine?

HEALTH FOR ALL?

You have been looking at how medicine and surgery have affected people in the rich parts of the world. But how do people in poorer parts of the world manage? And how do people get medical help when there are disasters like earthquakes?

There are international organisations that give emergency help and long-term support.

Factfile

The World Health Organisation (WHO)

This is part of the **United Nations**. It:

- gives people information about diseases like malaria and AIDS
- gives advice on the training of doctors, nurses and paramedics
- gives advice to governments on, for example, population control, childcare and sanitation
- undertakes research into, for example, the control of epidemics
- publishes technical papers by medical scientists.

What is it?

United Nations
This was set up before the end of the Second World War to try to keep peace in areas of war. Also it helps to stop disease and poverty worldwide. Most countries in the world have joined the UN.

The International Red Cross and Red Crescent

In times of war, these organisations help wounded soldiers and civilians as well as prisoners of war. In peacetime, these organisations help people affected by floods and famine, epidemics and earthquakes.

United Nations Children's Fund

- This is part of the United Nations.
- It is concerned with the welfare of children.
- It sets up basic healthcare programmes.
- It advises about nutrition for babies and children.
- It works with WHO on vaccination programmes. It has vaccinated 80 per cent of the world's children against diphtheria, measles, polio, tetanus, TB and whooping cough.

Medicins sans Frontières

This is the world's largest medical charity. It helps victims of war and natural disasters. It provides urgent medical and surgical care. It also provides clean water and sanitation.

All governments, no matter how poor, try to provide health care for their people. But this is often complicated by other factors. Here are some examples of these factors.

- **National pride.** Many countries in the world, particularly in Africa, were once ruled by western European powers. They now do not always want to accept help from their former rulers. They want to do things in their own way.
- **Priorities.** Some countries are busy fighting civil wars and do not have the spare cash for health care. Sometimes bandages and drugs given by aid agencies are taken by one side or the other.
- **Conflicting interests.** Aid organisations inside a country needing help sometimes argue with international aid agencies. They argue about what the help should be and who can give it faster.

Activity Time

1 Work in groups. You are going to create two imaginary families.

Family 1
- They live in Ethiopia, in a small village 80 kilometres from the nearest town.
- They have no electricity.
- The only water they have comes from one tap in the village.
- There are no flushing toilets and no sewerage system.
- There are no doctors or nurses in the village.
- The nearest hospital is 200 kilometres away.

Family 2
- They live in eastern Turkey.
- An earthquake has almost destroyed their small town.
- All the water mains and sewerage systems have been destroyed.
- Because of the earthquake, it is difficult to make contact with people from other parts of the world.

Each family should have parents, children and other relatives who might live with them or near them. Give everyone in your family a name and age that fits where they live.

2 See if you can work out the health risks that each family faces. You could put your information on a chart like this one. An example has been done for you.

Health risk	Is Family 1 at risk?	Is Family 2 at risk?
No sewerage.	✔	✔

3 Spend some time thinking about your two imaginary families. Then answer these questions.
a What help do they need?
b Where can they get this help?
c How can they make sure they stay healthy in the future?

HEALTH FOR ALL BY 2000?

The World Health Organisation says that everyone in the world has the right to the highest possible standard of health.

In 1981, 158 member countries of the World Health Organisation agreed that they would work for a 'Health for All' policy. They said there were eight goals they wanted everyone in the world to have by 2000.

1 Treatment of all common diseases and injuries.
2 Prevention and control of the main local diseases.
3 Provision of essential drugs.
4 Knowledge about proper nutrition and food supply.
5 Safe water supplies and basic sanitation.
6 Mother and child health care, including family planning.
7 Immunisation against the major infectious diseases.
8 Education about health problems.

Question Time

❶ Work in groups of four. Plan an answer to the question: 'Is "Health for All" really possible?'

a Each person in your group should choose two of the points above and work out how that point could be achieved.

b Put all the information from your group together.

c Decide how you are going to present it to the rest of the class. For example, you could:

• design an information poster
• write an account
• present a mock 'outside broadcast' by roving reporters.

Unit 21: From Aristotle to the atom – scientific discoveries that changed the world?

In this unit, we will look at discoveries that have changed the world. We will start with the big picture – the universe. We will end with the tiny picture – microbes and atoms.

The Earth as seen from space.

WHERE IS THE WORLD?

We know that our world is one of nine planets that circle the Sun. Our Sun is one of thousands of stars that make up the constellation we call the Milky Way. And the Milky Way is just one of thousands of constellations that make up the universe. We know all this because astronomers and scientists tell us so. Of course, this may all change when new discoveries in deep space are made.

WHAT DID EARLIER PEOPLE KNOW ABOUT THE UNIVERSE?

Thousands of years ago, people looked into deep space. They knew that the pattern of the stars changed.

SOURCE 2

It took several thousand years to build Stonehenge. It was finished around 2200BC. No one knows why it was built. **Archaeologists** believe that it was used for religious ceremonies, probably connected with the Sun and the stars. The midsummer sunrise and mid-winter sunset shine directly through two of the archways that you can see in the picture.

They knew that the Sun rose at one place on the horizon and set at another. They worked out theories to explain what was happening. Different peoples in different parts of the world had different theories. These theories changed as the centuries passed.

Who are they?

Archaeologist

Someone who studies remains of people and buildings that are extremely old (several thousand years).

SOURCE 3

About 400BC, the ancient Babylonians worked out a calendar. This told them when a new Moon would appear. The new Moon indicated the start of a new month.

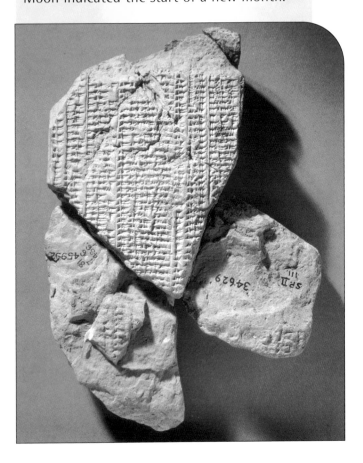

Question Time

1 Look at Sources 1 to 4. What does each source tell you about the ideas of the universe at the time?

SOURCE 4

This enormous circle was built by the American Indians. They believed that that the Sun, Earth and Moon were round and moved in circles.

ENTER ARISTOTLE!

Aristotle was a Greek **philosopher** who lived between 384 and 322BC. He had interesting views on just about everything. But what did he believe about the universe?

Aristotle, like everyone else, saw that the Sun rose in the east and set in the west. He saw that the planets and stars moved round the Earth. So, this is the way he thought the universe worked.

- The Earth was the centre of the universe.
- The Earth did not move.
- The stars and planets moved round the Earth.

Aristotle got it wrong. Some Greeks at the time thought he had got it wrong, too. But Aristotle was a well-respected teacher and thinker. Most people believed what he said. The Christian Church believed what he said. Aristotle had put God's creation (the Earth) at the centre of the universe and this, Christians believed, was the right and proper place for it to be. It was going to be hard to make the Church change its mind.

What does it mean?

Philosopher
Someone who thinks about big questions. The questions might be about God, or the Universe or the meaning of life.

This is the way Aristotle thought the universe worked. It is called a 'geocentric' universe because the Earth is at its centre.

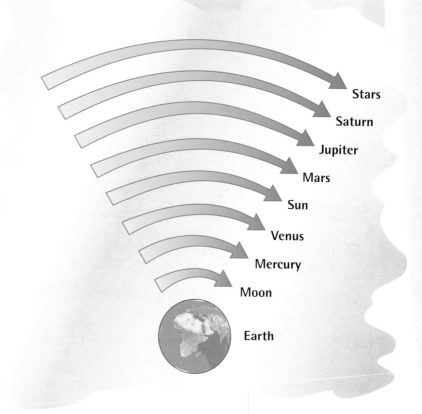

Stars
Saturn
Jupiter
Mars
Sun
Venus
Mercury
Moon

Earth

COPERNICUS' CHALLENGE

Nicolaus Copernicus (1473–1543) was a Polish astronomer.
He looked at the movements of the Sun, the
stars and the planets. The conclusions he drew
from what he saw were quite different from
those of Aristotle. This is the way Copernicus
thought the universe worked.

- The Earth went round the Sun, just like
  the other planets.
- The Earth took one year to travel
  round the Sun.
- As it went round the Sun, the
  Earth spun on its axis once
  every 24 hours.
- The Sun was fixed and did
  not move, even though it
  looked as if it moved.
- The stars were fixed and
  did not move, even
  though they looked as if
  they moved.

Copernicus' theory was
published in 1543. It was
going to cause great trouble for
the Church.

This is the way Copernicus thought
the universe worked. It is called
'heliocentric' because the Sun is at
its centre.

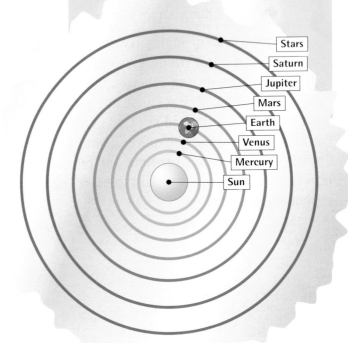

Stars
Saturn
Jupiter
Mars
Earth
Venus
Mercury
Sun

Question Time

1. Why did most people at the time believe in Aristotle's view
   of how the universe worked?

2. What were the basic differences between Aristotle's view of
   the universe and Copernicus' view?

3. Why would the Catholic Church be likely to disagree with
   Copernicus' view of the universe?

GALILEO GALILEI GETS IT RIGHT, TOO

An Italian, Galileo Galilei (1564–1642) was the first person to build and use telescopes to look at the Sun and Moon, the stars and the planets. What he saw convinced him that Copernicus was right. He saw everything Copernicus saw, and more. Galileo saw:

- moons going round the planet Jupiter
- Venus moving round the Sun.

This proved Copernicus was right and Aristotle was wrong.

Galileo published what he had discovered in *Sidereus Nuncius*, which means 'starry messenger'.

THE CATHOLIC CHURCH SUPPORTS ARISTOTLE!

Galileo was soon having big arguments with officials in the Catholic Church. They stuck to their belief that God's earth was the centre of the universe, and the Church then went further.

- It banned people from reading Copernicus' books.
- It also told Galileo that he was not to teach anything that might make people believe the Earth went round the Sun.

GALILEO ALLOWED TO WRITE

In 1624, Galileo began writing a book about the Moon and its relationship to the Earth. The Catholic Church gave him permission to write it. But when it was written, the book led to a lot of trouble.

GALILEO FOUND GUILTY OF HERESY

When Church officials read Galileo's book, they were horrified. It was clearly in favour of Copernicus' view of the universe. This went directly against Church teaching that the Earth was the centre of the universe. In 1632, Galileo was summoned to appear before the **Inquisition** in Rome. He was tried and found guilty of **heresy**. He was made to swear that:

- the Earth was the centre of the universe
- the Earth did not move.

Many Catholic churchmen believed Galileo was right. Indeed, the Catholic Church itself had used Copernicus' system to work out a new calendar! Most scientists knew Galileo was right. But it was not until 1992 that the Catholic Church apologised to him.

What does it mean?

The Inquisition

A group of Catholic churchmen. They were appointed by the Pope to make sure everyone obeyed the teachings of the Catholic Church. They questioned people who were accused of speaking or writing against the Church's teaching and could punish those found guilty. Sometimes, this punishment meant the people were put to death. Throughout the Catholic world, the Inquisition made people very frightened.

Heresy

Saying, writing or doing something that was opposed to the teachings of the Catholic Church.

SOURCE 5

This is a nineteenth-century painting of Galileo's trial in Rome.

Question Time

① Why did the Catholic Church try Galileo for heresy?

② Working in small groups, look carefully at Source 5, which is a painting of Galileo's trial.
a What do you think is happening?
b What is Galileo saying?
c What has the cardinal, dressed in red, been saying?

d What was the man in black, looking straight at you, thinking?
Write, and then act, a scene centred on this picture.

③ Look again at Source 5. It was painted about 300 years after Galileo's trial.
a Can we be sure the trial really looked like this?
b Explain your answer.

THE SCIENTIFIC REVOLUTION: WHAT IS A REVOLUTION?

THINKING ABOUT REVOLUTIONS

- Look back to the ideas and theories of Copernicus. What made them revolutionary?
- Think back to any work you might have done on the English Civil War. This is sometimes called the English Revolution. Can you work out why?
- The time when William and his wife Mary became king and queen of England is called the Glorious Revolution. Why was this a revolution?
- Think about any other revolutions you may have studied in history. You may, for example, have learned about:
  - the American Revolution
  - the French Revolution
  - the agricultural revolution
  - the industrial revolution.

What made people call these things 'revolutions'? Make a list of all the things that revolutions have in common. Make sure everyone else in your class agrees.

ISAAC NEWTON (1642–1727): A BOY PLAYING ON THE SEASHORE?

Isaac Newton was a Professor of Mathematics at Cambridge University. He began thinking about why planets kept in the same orbits round the Sun and didn't crash around in the sky.

This was the start of Newton's most important book *Mathematical Principles of Natural Philosophy*. In it, he explained why planets did not fall out of the sky, crash into each other or crash into the Sun. He showed there was a force, which he called gravity, that kept the planets apart. Gravity also affected everyday things. For example, it made apples fall to the ground.

The most important thing about Newton's theory was that it was universal. It could be applied anywhere, to anything. Newton's work was also important in two other ways.

- Other scientists began to look for universal laws for the branch of science they were working in.
- Newton showed scientists that experiments had to be repeated again and again, giving the same result, before they could claim that they proved something.

Isaac Newton made many other discoveries and inventions. Just before he died, he said, 'I do not know how I appear to the world, but to myself I seem only to have been a boy playing on the seashore, while the great ocean of truth lay all undiscovered before me.'

Question Time

❶ Copernicus discovered that the planets moved around (orbited) the Sun. Newton explained how this happened.
a Is it more important to discover something? Or is it more important to be able to explain why something happens?
b Explain your answer.

❷ Work in groups. You are going to research the lives and work of other people who were important in the scientific revolution of the seventeenth century. These people are:

- Francis Bacon
- Robert Hooke
- Richard Lower
- Robert Boyle
- William Harvey
- Charles II

This is what you need to find out about each person:
- what their discoveries or inventions were
- why they were important
- how they affected people at the time
- how they affected people later.
Think about how you can present what you have found out to the rest of the class.

❸ Think about what revolution means. Look at page 201 to give you some ideas.
a Do you think there was a scientific revolution in the seventeenth century?
b Explain your answer.

MAKING CONNECTIONS

Aristotle, Copernicus and Newton were all concerned with:

- how the planets moved
- how the stars moved
- how the Sun moved
- how the Moon moved
- where the Earth was in all this.

CHARLES DARWIN: ARE PEOPLE JUST ANOTHER SPECIES?

Nineteenth century Britain was one of great contrasts. Look at the two pictures in Sources 1 and 2.

SOURCE 1

This picture from the nineteenth century shows an engine (*The Rocket*) that was built by George and Robert Stephenson. George and Robert went on to build miles of railway track and many engines.

SOURCE 2

In 1851 the Great Exhibition was held in the Crystal Palace, London. The exhibition was designed to show the greatest achievements of the different countries in the world. This is a picture of the British section.

Question Time

Look at Sources 1 and 2. What words would you use to describe the people who lived in a society like this? Choose two words from the ones below and explain why.

enterprising   adventurous   curious   clever   technical

dangerous   inventive   brave   creative   rich

Now look at Sources 3, 4 and 5.

SOURCE 3

The cover of a book about the life and achievements of Dr David Livingstone (1813–73). He was a missionary and an explorer.

SOURCE 4

An engraving of the Temple Church in about 1830. The Temple Church was a fashionable London church at the time. You won't see any poor people in this picture!

SOURCE 5

This is a photograph of the beach at Hastings in 1888. You can see a line of bathing machines along the beach. People undressed in the bathing machines, which were then pushed into the sea. People opened the doors and swam into the sea. In this way, people could swim without anyone seeing their bare arms or legs.

Question Time

Look at Sources 3, 4 and 5. What words would you use to describe people who lived in a society like this? Choose two words from the ones below and explain why you have chosen them?

conservative   rigid   conformist   proud
conventional   traditional   respectable
sensible   strait-laced   proper

THE VOYAGE OF THE *BEAGLE*

In December 1831, the ship HMS *Beagle* set sail for South America. On board was a young **naturalist** called Charles Darwin (1809–82). He was going to study the birds and animals there. What he saw, and his theories about what he saw, were to change forever the way most people thought about the human race.

What do they do?

Naturalist
Someone who studies natural history (things to do with plants and people).

Before Charles Darwin worked out his theories, what did people believe about the beginnings of life on Earth?

- Most **geologists** believed in the catastrophe theory. They believed that there had been creations of different types of animals and plants (the dinosaurs, for example) and then something terrible had happened to wipe them out. They believed animals and plants didn't change at all between being created and being wiped out.
- A British geologist, Charles Lyall, was beginning to think that perhaps the Earth's surface and everything on it had been changing ever since God created the world. Lyall called this change 'evolution'.

When Charles Darwin went on his journey, he took a book that Lyall had written about evolution. Darwin knew that at least one other person was thinking the same things as he was.

Darwin was particularly interested in the animal life he found on the Galapagos Islands, 1000 kilometres off the coast of Ecuador in South America. Each island had its own types of birds and animals. However, there were some things that were the same about them all. He began to wonder what had made the differences.

What do they do?

Geologist
Someone who studies what the Earth's surface is made of.

ON THE ORIGIN OF SPECIES, 1859

In 1859, Charles Darwin wrote a book about what he had seen and what he thought about what he had seen. This is what he said.

- There is not enough food to go round. Therefore, every animal will struggle to survive.
- Those that are successful in the struggle will have special variations – longer necks or stronger beaks, for example. Because they survive, they will pass on these variations to their offspring.
- The species that are unsuccessful will die out.
- This process takes thousands of years.

WHY DID THIS CAUSE SUCH AN UPSET IN VICTORIAN BRITAIN?

Darwin's views made people re-think their beliefs for three main different reasons.

- The Bible says that God created the world in six days. But Darwin said that animals and plants took thousands of years to evolve. He was saying the Bible was wrong.
- Darwin's picture of the ways in which animals and plants evolved is one of struggle and death. But Christians believe in a loving God and this didn't seem to agree with what Darwin was saying.
- Darwin's theories meant that people were the same as other animals and had not been specially made by God. In 1871 Darwin wrote a book called *The Descent of Man* which explained how humans evolved.

WHAT WERE VICTORIAN PEOPLE'S ATTITUDES TO DARWIN AND HIS THEORIES?

Look at Sources 6, 7 and 8. What attitude to Darwin's theories does each source show?

SOURCE 6

Man has control over the Earth. He can speak and think sensibly. He can choose what he does. He is made in the image of God. This cannot be matched up with the terrible idea that Man had animal beginnings.

This is how Samuel Wilberforce reacted to Darwin's *On the Origin of Species* . Wilberforce was the Bishop of Oxford.

SOURCE 7

This cartoon was published in 1874. It is called 'As others see us'.

SOURCE 8

It is possible to believe in a God who has created animals and plants that are capable of developing and changing. It is just as possible to do this, as it is to believe in a God who made each species separately that didn't change at all.

This is part of a letter Charles Kingsley wrote to Charles Darwin. Charles Kingsley was a university professor and a Christian.

Question Time

Look back to Sources 4 and 5. What impact do you think Darwin's theories would have had on the people in these pictures?

THE LONDON SKETCH BOOK.

PROF. DARWIN.

This is the ape of form.
Love's Labor Lost, act 5, scene 2.

Some four or five descents since.
All's Well that Ends Well, act 3, sc. 7.

MIASMA OR GERMS: HOW IS DISEASE SPREAD?

Think back to two frightening killer diseases you have learned about in history lessons: the Black Death and cholera.

The diseases had a lot in common.

- They spread rapidly.
- They had frightening symptoms.
- They killed a lot of people very quickly.

But the two most important thing that linked them were that:

- nobody knew what caused the diseases, and
- no one knew how they spread.

HOW DID PEOPLE THINK DISEASE SPREAD?

Sources 1 to 4 will give you some idea of what people thought were the causes of disease.

SOURCE 1

We took Plutus to a temple where there were a lot of sick people with all kinds of illnesses. We put our gifts to the gods on the altar. The temple priest put out the light and told us to go to sleep. Then the god sat down by Plutus and wiped his eyes. Next, the god's daughter covered Plutus' face with some red cloth.

The god whistled and two huge snakes appeared. They crept under the cloth and licked Plutus' eyes. Plutus sat up and could see again. But the god and his helpers had disappeared.

From *Plutus*, a play written by Aristophanes. He was a Greek playwright who died in 388BC. Here he tells how Plutus was cured by the gods.

SOURCE 4

The stink from plague sores poisons and corrupts the air. It is best to flee from infected people.

In times of plague, people should not crowd together, because someone might be infected.

All stinks should be avoided – stables, stinking fields, paths and streets, carcasses and stinking waters.

Let your house be clean and make a clear fire of flaming wood. Chase out the evil smells with herbs, bay leaves, juniper and oregano.

Written in 1485 by the Bishop of Aarhus, in Denmark.

SOURCE 2

Here is the great cure! Come! You who drive evil things from my stomach and my limbs. He who drinks this shall be cured, just as the gods in the skies were cured.

Doctors in ancient Egypt (about 1500BC) chanted this spell while giving medicine to their patients.

SOURCE 3

If the pain is under your ribs, clear your bowels with medicine made from black hellebore, cumin or other fragrant herbs.

A bath will help pneumonia, because it soothes the pain and brings up phlegm. The bather must keep quiet and do nothing himself. The pouring of water and the rubbing must be left to others.

The Greek philosopher, Hippocrates (460-377BC) believed that a person's body had to be in perfect balance if they were to be healthy.

Activity Time

1 Work with a partner. Read Sources 1 to 4 carefully.
a Work out what the 'cure' was in each source.
b Have a guess at what the illness was in each source.
You could put your answers on a chart like this one.

Source	The cure	The illness
Source 1		
Source 2		

2 What do these sources tell us about medical knowledge at the time?

HOW DID DISEASE SPREAD?

By 1800, people had two main theories (ideas) about how disease spread.

- Miasmas. These were invisible gases that caused disease and spread it through the air.
- Spontaneous generation. Decaying things turned into maggots and germs that spread disease.

Scientists wondered about the theory of spontaneous generation. They could see maggots growing out of dead flesh. They looked down microscopes and saw rotting meat teeming with micro-organisms (germs). Maybe the theory was correct. Maybe decaying matter did cause disease. But what if it was the other way round? What if the germs caused the decay and were not caused by decay?

ENTER LOUIS PASTEUR

Louis Pasteur (1822–95) was Professor of Chemistry at Lille University, in France. He set up a lot of experiments that proved micro-organisms (germs) caused beer to go bad. The bad beer did not make the germs. Germs made the beer go bad.

SOURCE 5

I place some liquid in a flask with a long neck. I boil it and let it cool. In a few days, little animals will grown in it.

If I repeat the experiment, but draw the neck into a curve, but still open, the liquid will remain pure for three or four years.

What difference is there between them? They both contain the same liquid and they both contain air. The difference is that, in one, the dust in the air and the germs in it can fall in. In the other, they cannot.

Pasteur describes the experiment he carried out in public in Paris in 1864.

In 1865, Pasteur went one step further. He had already made the link between germs and decay. He set up some more experiments, investigating a disease among silkworms. These made the vital link between germs and disease.

KOCH CONTINUES THE WORK

Robert Koch (1843–1910) was a German doctor and a scientific researcher. He set out to discover the particular germs that caused particular diseases. He found the germs that caused **anthrax**, **septicaemia**, tuberculosis and **cholera**.

By 1900, Robert Koch had identified the germs causing 21 separate diseases. This meant that it would now be possible to cure these diseases.

What is it?

Anthrax
A disease that sheep and cattle can catch.

Septicaemia
Blood poisoning.

Cholera
A disease that can often lead to death. People who live in areas with poor sanitation can get cholera.

SOURCE 6

In the twentieth century, the government published a lot of information posters like this one.

MINISTRY OF HEALTH SAYS–

COUGHS AND SNEEZE SPREAD DISEASES–

trap the germs in your handkerchief

HELP TO KEEP THE NATION FIGHTING

Question Time

❶ What was the 'spontaneous generation' theory? As a clue, look back to page 211.

❷ What was Louis Pasteur's 'germ theory'? As a clue, look back to page 211.

❸ How did Louis Pasteur's germ theory prove that the theory of spontaneous generation was wrong?

❹ Why was the germ theory so important?

❺ In the fight against disease who was more important:
a Louis Pasteur or Robert Koch?
b Explain why you think this.

Activity Time

Make a poster that could have come from the 1880s. The poster should encourage people to protect themselves from the spread of disease by germs.

SPLITTING THE ATOM: FOR GOOD OR ILL?

WHERE DID THIS ENORMOUS POWER COME FROM?

The power of an atomic bomb comes from splitting the nucleus of certain types of uranium or plutonium atoms. This splitting results in a huge and devastating explosion.

WHO SPLIT THE ATOM AND WHEN WAS THE ATOMIC BOMB DEVELOPED?

1932   John Cockcroft and Ernest Walton split the atom.

1938   Many of Europe's leading scientists fled to Britain or the USA as war approached.

1942   The top secret American Manhattan Project designed and built the first atomic bomb.

BUT ...

The Allies knew German nuclear scientists were working on a nuclear bomb, too.

SOURCE 1

An atomic bomb explodes.

All the scientists working in nuclear physics knew of the immense power released by splitting the atom. One of them, Albert Einstein, wrote to the President of the USA to warn him.

SOURCE 2

This recent work could lead to the construction of bombs. In view of this, you may think it sensible to keep in close contact with the government and with the scientists who are working on nuclear chain reactions.

I understand that Germany has stopped selling uranium from Czechoslovakian mines, and that in Berlin some of the American work on uranium is being copied.

Part of a letter from Albert Einstein to Franklin D Roosevelt, written in August 1939.

- The first atomic bomb was tested in the USA on 16 July 1945.
- On 6 August 1945 an atomic bomb was exploded over the Japanese city of Hiroshima.
- On 9 August 1945 an atomic bomb was exploded over the Japanese city of Nagasaki.

Question Time

❶ Read Source 2.
a What is Albert Einstein saying about an atomic bomb?
b What is he saying about Germany?

❷ What would you guess President Roosevelt's reaction to be? (Clue: look at the date and think about the Second World War.)

❸ Usually, scientists make the discoveries and politicians make the decisions about how these discoveries should be used.
a Do you think this is right?
b Explain your answer.

WHY DID ALLIED LEADERS DECIDE TO DROP THE ATOMIC BOMB IN 1945?

Read Sources 3 to 6. Then try to decide why allied leaders dropped the atomic bomb in 1945.

SOURCE 3

To force Japan to surrender may take over a million American and British lives. The Japanese people think it is a disgrace to surrender. They might find the sight of this powerful weapon an excuse that would save their honour. They might no longer think they had to fight to the last man.

The explanation for dropping the bomb given by the British Prime Minister, Winston Churchill, in 1945.

SOURCE 4

I told the President that I was extremely worried for two reasons.

First, I believed that Japan was about to surrender. So dropping the bomb was completely unnecessary.

Second, I thought the USA should not shock world opinion by using a weapon that was no longer essential to save American lives.

General Eisenhower, the Supreme Allied Commander in Europe, describes his reaction to the decision of President Truman of the USA to drop the bomb.

SOURCE 5

We thought of the fighting men who would be sent to invade Japan. We thought about the number of American and Japanese lives that would be lost. We were determined to find a way to show Japan just how powerful the bomb was, and we wanted to do this without loss of life. If only this could be done.

This was said by Arthur Compton, who was a member of a committee that looked at US weapons policy.

SOURCE 6

My own view is that the evidence we have shows that the atomic bomb was not needed to end the war and to save lives. My view is also that the American leaders knew this.

Written by Gar Alperovitz in his book *Atomic Diplomacy: Hiroshima and Potsdam*, published in 1965.

NUCLEAR POWER: FOR OR AGAINST?

The knowledge of how to split the atom and of the enormous power this produced could not be lost or forgotten.

NUCLEAR WEAPONS

- The USA developed nuclear weapons because it was afraid Germany would do so first and so win the Second World War.
- The USSR built nuclear weapons because it was afraid of the nuclear power of the USA.
- Britain and France built nuclear weapons because they were afraid of the nuclear power of the USSR.
- This 'arms race' became an important part of the Cold War between the superpowers, the USA and the USSR, in the second half of the twentieth century.
- More and more powerful weapons were built by both sides. But did they make the world a safer place?

Question Time

1 Read Sources 3 to 6.
a What reasons do the writers give to say that the bomb should be dropped?
b What reasons do the writers give to say that the bomb should not be dropped?

2 Look at the people who wrote the sources. Look also at when the sources were written.
a Why do you think these people thought what they did?
b Why are the dates of the sources important?

3 Do you think that the decision to drop the atomic bomb was the correct one to take at the time? Explain your answer.

POWER IN DAILY LIFE

- Some scientists worked to use nuclear power for peaceful ends. They worked to turn this power into electricity.

BUT ...

- Many people are worried about the dangers of building and operating nuclear power plants.

Other people are glad that a source of energy has been found that does not pollute the Earth with carbon dioxide – one of the gases responsible for global warming.

SOURCE 7

This is the Sizewell nuclear power plant in Suffolk, England. In Britain, nuclear power plants began working in 1956.

SOURCE 8

In 1986 the nuclear power plant at Chernobyl in the USSR exploded. The nuclear fall-out reached 20 countries, including Britain.

Scientists think that up to 5 million people will eventually die as a result. This picture shows decontamination trucks rushing to the explosion.

SOURCE 9

Many people object to the very existence of nuclear weapons. The Campaign for Nuclear Disarmament (CND) provides information and organises marches and protests.

Question Time

1 Find out about the different ways in which people have developed and used nuclear power since 1945. Work in groups and use Sources 7 to 9 as your starting point. Use your school library and the Internet.

2 Now use the information you have collected to make a case either for or against the use of nuclear power in the twenty-first century

3 Decide how you are going to present your case to others. You could, for example:
- design a website, or
- make a poster, or
- design and print a leaflet using computer-aided design.

WHICH DISCOVERIES CHANGED THE WORLD THE MOST?

Activity Time

ENTER THE BALLOON – AND LEAVE IT!

Working in groups, decide which person in this unit you think made the most important discovery of all time, and why.

Now – in your imagination! – put the person chosen by your group and the people chosen by the other groups in your class into a hot air balloon. Make sure all the groups have chosen someone different.

The hot air balloon has been sailing well for some time. Suddenly, it begins to sink towards the ground. People have to be thrown out to keep the balloon in the air. Who will be the last in the balloon, and so survive?

Make a case for your historical person staying in the balloon until the end – and argue it in front of your class.

Debate – argue – and decide!

Unit 22: The role of the individual – for good or ill?

WHY ARE CERTAIN PEOPLE 'FAMOUS'?

You have been learning about the past and finding out about people we call 'famous'. Have you ever thought about these interesting questions?

- Why are some people famous while others are not?
- Why do we remember some people but forget others?
- What do we choose to remember about these famous people?
- Does what we think about famous people change over time?

You will explore some of these ideas before going on to study three famous people in history. We are not just interested in the people themselves but with the more difficult questions of how and why they are remembered as they are.

Activity Time

A THINKING ABOUT BEING FAMOUS

Famous people of the twenty-first century

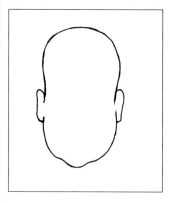 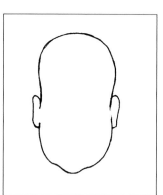

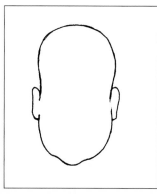 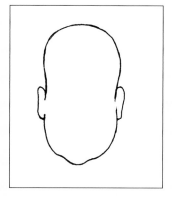

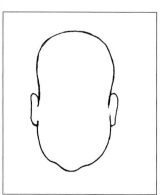 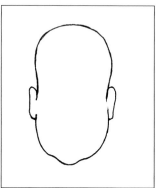

There are no pictures in the boxes opposite. This is because you are going to choose them.

1 **a** Make six cards like the ones shown. Write in the names of six famous people who are alive today. Be original and choose carefully.

b In small groups, compare your cards of famous people. Sort all the famous people into different groups. Your groups could include:
- jobs – for example, pop star, politician, sportsperson, scientist
- good things they have done
- bad things they have done.

c Make a note of the two most popular types of famous people chosen by your group.

d Now draw in the faces of your own cards (if you can!) and write underneath the main reason why each person is famous.

2 **a** Now make a list of six famous people from the past. In your small group sort out these new names into different groups (as before).

b What are the two most popular types of famous person chosen by your group from the past?

c Compare the types of people you have chosen from the past and from today. What similarities are there? What differences are there?

3 All your choices of famous people say something about you and your society. Use the questions below to discuss what your choices say about you.
- What kind of people are looked up to by people like you?
- What sort of things (race, sex, job, family, wealth, good or bad deeds) make a difference to who becomes famous today?

4 To show how the answers to these questions can change from generation to generation, now ask an older person (you decide how old!) to write down the names of three famous people from today and three from the past.

a Ask the older person the reason for their choices. Write this down.

b What similarities are there to your choices?

c What differences are there?

d Can you give any reasons why some choices might be the same and others might be different? Write down these reasons.

You are now going to find out about three famous people:

- one from the Middle Ages
- one from the eighteenth century, and
- one from the twentieth century.

WHO WAS ELEANOR OF AQUITAINE?

Our first person is Eleanor of Aquitaine, a powerful queen.

PERSONNEL FILE

Birth	1122 in Bordeaux, France. Her father was the Duke of Aquitaine. He ruled part of France.
Education	Took place at her father's court. Eleanor learned to read and write in Latin. She also learned several languages.
Marriage	1137 Eleanor married Louis, the French prince. He later became king. After giving birth to two daughters, Eleanor's marriage was annulled (cancelled) in 1152. Later in 1152 she married Henry of Anjou. He became King Henry II of England. They had five sons and three daughters.
Job	Queen to two very powerful kings. Mother of two English kings – Richard the Lionheart and John. Patron (sponsor) of poets, musicians and writers. A power builder.
Famous events in life	When her father died, Eleanor was 15 years old. She took over ruling his kingdom. She became Queen of France and then Queen of England. She helped her husbands rule. While Queen of France, Eleanor went on a Crusade with her husband King Louis. It was almost unheard of for a woman to go on Crusade. In the 1170s Eleanor plotted with her children to overthrow and possibly even murder her husband, King Henry II. She was caught and locked up by Henry for 16 years until he died. When she was free from prison, she was in her sixties. She helped her sons Richard and John to become more powerful.
Death	In 1204 at the age of 82.

Eleanor's life story tells us about many aspects of medieval life – royal politics, marriage, travel around Europe, contact with the Arabs, the **Crusades**, religions, music and poetry. Eleanor was a special women for her time.

Question Time

❶ Write a short paragraph describing what sort of woman Eleanor of Aquitaine was. Use describing words like 'determined' or 'clever', rather than just saying what she did.

❷ Make a list of what made Eleanor special for her time.

SOURCE 1

Eleanor's tomb at Fontevrault Abbey. To the left was her husband Henry II and her son Richard I.

EARLY LIFE OF ELEANOR

At the age of 15, when her father died, Eleanor's life changed. She became ruler of the Duchy of Aquitaine and Poitiers. Her kingdom covered half of present-day France. In the same year Eleanor married Louis, **heir** to the French throne. She became Queen of France.

What does it mean?

The Crusades
Holy Wars. They began in the eleventh century.

Heir
Next in line to be king or queen.

People at the French court who knew Eleanor said she was clever, beautiful and fun. Eleanor was often described as having long dark hair and bright, sparkling eyes. Her husband, Louis, was described as a dull man.

When the Second Crusade began, Eleanor insisted on going with Louis to the Middle East. She also took 300 of her women servants. This decision shocked people. The Pope was so horrified that he banned any women from going on the next Crusade.

LOVE AFFAIRS

- Rumours started to spread that Eleanor had lovers while she was on Crusade.
- During the Crusade Eleanor started to find out about how to have her marriage annulled (cancelled). It was clear that she and Louis did not get on well. Eleanor is supposed to have complained: 'I have married a monk rather than a king!'
- Eleanor gave birth to two daughters. She left her daughters to be brought up at the French court. This was not unusual in the Middle Ages.

ELEANOR AND HENRY II

Eleanor soon found herself a new husband, Henry of Anjou. She was 30 and he was 19 when they met. Henry did not behave like a monk at all! He was very good looking and well educated. He was also determined to get more power, land and money. Eleanor and Henry seemed well matched.

Question Time

❶ Eleanor insisted on going on Crusades. What does this tell us about her character?

❷ Why do you think the marriage between Eleanor and Louis failed? Look at the possible reasons. You can pick more than one.
a It failed because of rumours that Eleanor had lovers.
b It failed because Eleanor gave birth to daughters, not sons.
c It failed because Eleanor and Louis had different ideas and different personalities.

❸ Eleanor left her young daughters to be brought up at King Louis' court.
a Do you think this action was selfish and cruel, or clever and selfless? Or have you come to a different conclusion?
b Explain your answer.

Their marriage meant that Henry would rule over Eleanor's French kingdom. This made Louis angry, because he and Henry were rivals. In 1154 Henry also became Henry II, King of England. Eleanor was his queen.

Eleanor and Henry lived mostly in Westminster Palace in London but Henry liked travelling around their kingdom. While he was away Eleanor ruled for him. She also gave birth to eight children, but this did not stop her travelling too.

SOURCE 2

Eleanor saw Henry as the future King of England. She also saw him as a young man, full of adventure.

Henry saw Eleanor as the chance for a brilliant political partnership, because she owned more than half of France.

A modern historian describing the marriage of Eleanor and Henry.

A map of Europe and the Holy Land. It shows the important places in Eleanor's life.

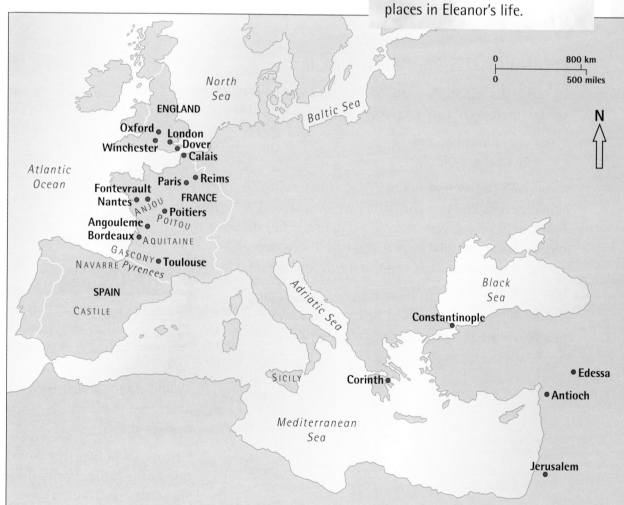

Question Time

Look at the map on page 225.

1 Point out:
   a land that Eleanor inherited from her father
   b Henry's land in France.

2 Why do you think Henry wanted to marry Eleanor?

3 Why do you think Eleanor wanted to marry Henry?

4 List two reasons why Eleanor's marriage to Henry was successful, and two reasons why her marriage to Louis was not.

ELEANOR: A WOMAN OF POWER

Eleanor had learned a lot about politics in Louis' French court. This experience helped her to increase the power of her sons and she became a clever politician. Eleanor and Henry gained more power in several ways.

- They took over ruling Ireland and parts of France.
- They organised good marriages for their children.

ELEANOR PLOTS AGAINST HENRY II

By the 1170s, Eleanor's marriage to Henry was starting to go wrong. There were two main reasons:

- personal problems, and
- family rivalry.

It was well known that Henry II was unfaithful to Eleanor. In fact, he had several children with other women. One of his lovers, Rosamund Clifford, was actually living in a set of rooms in the royal home in Oxford. Henry II also had a very bad temper – remember what happened to Thomas Becket.

Henry II found it hard to share his power, especially with his eldest son, also called Henry. Father and son argued over what lands they each should rule.

SOURCE 3

Don't you know that it is our nature from our ancestors that none of us should love each other, and brothers should fight against each other and son fight against father.

Eleanor's son Geoffrey wrote this to his father Henry II about the tradition of fighting in the family.

Eleanor took the side of her sons against Henry. She helped to protect young Henry when he rebelled against his father in 1173. Eleanor went as far as leading a rebellion of her sons against Henry II.

Some time later, Eleanor was caught by Henry II. She was said to be disguised as a man. Eleanor was kept prisoner by Henry for the next 16 years until he died. It took Henry ten years to finally squash the rebellions against him by his own children.

Question Time

1 Do you and the person sitting next to you agree about what Geoffrey is saying to his father in Source 2? Discuss your ideas.

2 Why do you think Eleanor led a rebellion against her husband? Answer this question using two spider diagrams:
- one with answers about revenge
- the other with answers about power.

3 Write a one-minute news report about the rebellion against Henry II. Include:
- the role Eleanor played
- why she plotted against Henry II
- one other main point of your own.

ELEANOR: EUROPEAN WOMAN

In 1189 Henry II died. Eleanor's favourite son, Richard, took over as King. Eleanor was set free. Even though she was in her sixties she was full of energy. The 1190s were an exciting new stage in her life.

- Between 1190 and 1194 she ruled England for Richard I while he was on Crusade. When Richard was caught and locked up on his way home from the Holy Land, Eleanor organised the huge ransom for him to be set free.
- Eleanor continued to increase the power of her family. She made sure they made good marriages.
- Eleanor even rode over the Pyrenees mountains at the age of 70 to collect a princess to marry Richard.

In 1204 Eleanor died while spending some time in prayer and reflection at the Abbey at Fontevrault. She was 82 and had lived a full and exciting life.

Activity Time

1 You are a Hollywood film producer. You think Eleanor's life history would make a great story for a film. Create an eight-frame storyboard of her life.
a Pick eight events from this section that, together, will make a great story.
b Draw and label each frame on your storyboard to describe an event. Make sure that you tell your story in date order.

c Write a short paragraph for the film trailer, which explains why people today will be interested in Eleanor's story. Mention what they will find:

- exciting
- inspiring
- sad
- important, and so on.

HOW HAS ELEANOR BEEN PORTRAYED?

In a recent biography of Eleanor, an historian said that Eleanor attracted legends to herself like metal to a magnet. In other words, she was the type of woman who people talked about both during her lifetime and long after her death. Although not all of the stories told about Eleanor are true, they are still interesting and important to historians. The stories tell us about what people thought important and interesting at different times in the past.

ELEANOR THE AMAZON WOMAN

You will remember that when Eleanor decided to go on Crusade with her husband Louis and 300 of her women servants, she shocked the world. Both at the time and later, Eleanor was compared to an Amazon woman.

'Amazon' women were said to have lived in Ancient Greece. They were tall, strong and fit warriors, and they were said to have cut off their right breasts so they could use their bows and arrows more easily.

229

SOURCE 1

A picture of Eleanor of Aquitaine as she arrived in Constantinople on Crusade in 1147. It is from a book published in 1989.

SOURCE 2

Even women travelled in their ranks, boldly sitting in their saddles as men do, dressed in male clothes and, with their lances and armour, looking just like men.

With their warlike looks, they behaved in an even more masculine way than the Amazons.

A description of the Second Crusade arriving in Constantinople. It was written soon after the event.

The description in Source 2 was written by a Greek historian. He does not mention Eleanor by name. But he is probably describing her and her servants.

A female historian from the Victorian period, called Agnes Strickland, also wrote about the event. As you read Source 3, ask yourself what Agnes thinks of Eleanor.

SOURCE 3

Queen Eleanor put on the dress of an Amazon. Her ladies surrounded her. On the Crusade King Louis showed great courage. But he was saddled with this army of women. The freaks of Queen Eleanor and her female warriors were the cause of all the problems of King Louis and his army. For example, the king was slowed down by the huge amount of baggage that Eleanor and her servants insisted on taking on Crusade.

Agnes Strickland's description of Eleanor on Crusade.

Question Time

1 Do Sources 1 and 2 agree about what Eleanor wore on Crusade?

a Does Source 2 actually say that Eleanor dressed as an Amazon woman?
b Why do you think that people jumped to the conclusion that they wore Amazonian clothes?

Source	What Eleanor wore
Source 1	She wore ...
Source 2	She wore ...

2 Read Source 3 again. Pick out three words or phrases that show what Agnes Strickland thought of Eleanor.

3 Agnes was writing in Victorian times about Eleanor. Which of these sentences best explains why Agnes did not approve of Eleanor? Discuss your ideas in pairs.

a Agnes agreed with many Victorians that women should not be involved in politics.
b Agnes just did not like Eleanor as a person.
c Agnes was writing hundreds of years after Eleanor was alive.
d Agnes did not like the new women's rights movement that was growing in Victorian times.

ELEANOR AND SALAH AL-DEEN – A MEDIEVAL SCANDAL!

One of the best stories about Eleanor was of her affair with a great Arab leader. His name was Salah al-Deen. You may have heard him called Saladin. In 1186, Salah al-Deen went to war against the Christians and captured Jerusalem a year later. It is unlikely that this scandal is true.

Why did people at the time think it was a good story?
Arabic life, art and ideas were fashionable in the Middle Ages. The Arabs were the big enemies of the Christians during the Crusades. The courts in Europe loved to hear stories from the Middle East, especially a story that brought the two sides together in a love affair.

Question Time

1 **a** When did Eleanor go on Crusade?
b When did Salah al-Deen go to war against the Christians?
c Do you believe that the story of their love affair is true? Explain your answer.

2 Can you think of another reason why it is unlikely to be a true story?

3 What sort of people do we gossip about in Britain today? Pop stars, politicians – who else?

4 How different is this to Eleanor's time?

ELEANOR: WOMAN OF CULTURE

Eleanor has not just been described as a scandalous woman who was greedy for power. She has also been described as a woman important to Medieval poetry, writing and music.

Her court in Aquitaine was a famous centre for the arts. Love songs and poems were very popular. Eleanor encouraged women as well as men to write poetry and songs, which was unusual at that time.

SOURCE 4

Fair, sweet lover, how will you cope without me out on the salty sea,

When nothing could ever tell the grief in my heart?

When I think of your gentle, sparkling face that I used to kiss and touch,

It is a miracle that I am not mad.

These lyrics were written by a woman whose lover had gone on Crusade.

Question Time

❶ Work in pairs. Make up three news headlines about Eleanor that might appear in a gossip magazine or tabloid newspaper.

❷ What is it about Eleanor that makes people want to write about her? Your answer should be two paragraphs long:
  • one about Eleanor's private life, and
  • the other about her political life.

❸ Discuss in pairs two reasons that explain how untrue stories are sometimes told about people in the past.

WHAT IMPACT DID ELEANOR HAVE BOTH DURING HER LIFETIME AND AFTER?

Eleanor experienced a lot of things in her lifetime. This was partly because of her wealth and powerful position. But also it was because she had a determined character. Eleanor had far more experience than most medieval women.

What ideas did people have about women in the twelfth century?

- Women were mainly thought of as mothers and wives.
- The Church said that women should not be totally trusted, because in the Bible Eve had tempted Adam.

Because of these ideas it was not thought proper for women to travel or have power. It was unusual for women to be involved in politics. Eleanor was not typical of her time.

Question Time

❶ List three separate words that describe how women were seen in the early Middle Ages.

❷ Think of three ways in which Eleanor's life was different to medieval ideas about women.

WHO WAS DICK TURPIN? WAS HIS STORY FACT OR FICTION?

Our second individual also has many legends about him. He is a folk hero. This means that stories about him were passed down through generations. These stories often change each time they are told. Every society has legends. These can be about people who have done bad things as well as good. Sometimes the stories about the 'baddies' are better and the people become heroes.

Source 1 shows a late twentieth-century 'baddie'. His name was Ronnie Biggs. He was a thief. In 1963 he and his gang robbed a train. They stole £2,600,000.

SOURCE 1

Ronnie Biggs holding the poster published by the British police after the train robbery. The photograph was taken in 1994 in Brazil, where Biggs was hiding.

At first the train robbers got away with their crime. But then they were caught and sent to prison. After a few months, Biggs escaped. He went to live in Brazil. The British police could not capture him there.

The money the train robbers stole was never found. Ronnie Biggs is a thief, an escaped convict and he owes Britain a lot of money. Why do you think his story is so popular?

In the future people may remember Biggs in films or songs and poems. Dick Turpin is a 'baddie' from the past who has been remembered like this.

PERSONNEL FILE

Birth	1706 in Essex.
Education	Trained as a butcher.
Marriage	To Mary Millington.
Occupation	Butcher, thief, murderer and highwayman!
Famous events in life	1734 Turpin was part of the 'Gregory Gang'. The gang robbed farmhouses and used violence against their victims. 1735 The Gregory Gang collapsed after several members were caught and hanged. 1737 Turpin joined up with highwayman Tom King and robbed people in the south of England. King was caught, but Turpin hid in a forest. He then shot a gamekeeper and rode to the north of England to avoid being caught. Legend says that he covered 190 miles in less than a day on his horse, Black Bess.
Death	1739 In Yorkshire Turpin changed his name. But he was eventually arrested and his real identity was discovered. He was put on trial and hanged in York.

Dick Turpin on his horse, Black Bess. The story of his brave ride from London to York is the most famous one about him.

DICK TURPIN *Clearing the Old Hornsey toll bar* GATE,
TO THE SURPRISE OF HIS PURSUERS.

THE LIFE OF A HIGHWAYMAN IN THE EIGHTEENTH CENTURY

The eighteenth century was a good time to be a highwayman. England was becoming one of the wealthiest countries in the world. More people had more money and people carried their money with them when they travelled. Travel was getting easier, because roads were improving. England was full of big forests, perfect for jumping out on travellers and hiding in afterwards.

Question Time

❶ Why did large forests and better roads make life better for highwaymen in the eighteenth century?

❷ Look at Source 2. What is Turpin doing that shows him to be brave and reckless?

❸ How do other people in Source 2 react to Turpin? Look at their faces and what they are doing.

❹ Does Source 2 give a positive or negative image of Turpin? Explain your answer.

MORE ABOUT DICK TURPIN

Early crimes

- As a young man, Turpin set up a butcher's shop in London. He started to sell deer stolen by poachers.
- He was caught stealing cattle and ran off to the Essex countryside.
- He joined the Gregory Gang. They broke into isolated farmhouses and terrorised people until they gave up their money.
- Once, Turpin broke into the house of an old woman because he had heard she had £700 in her house. He hung her over the fire until she told him where the money was kept.

Fame and violence

By 1735, the *London Evening Post* newspaper had regular reports on Turpin. The King offered a £50 reward for the capture of the Gregory Gang. The gang broke into the house of a rich farmer. They beat the farmer and his family until they got their treasures. Turpin escaped by jumping out of a window.

Partners in crime

Turpin hid in East Anglia and joined up with a famous highwayman Tom King. Together they robbed travellers. But King was arrested. Turpin tried to shoot the policeman, but shot King instead. Turpin hid in a forest where he shot a gamekeeper to avoid being caught.

As John Palmer in Yorkshire

Turpin went to Yorkshire where he called himself 'John Palmer'. When 'Palmer' was arrested for a small crime, his real identity was given away.

Caught at last

Turpin was put on trial and sentenced to death. He gave all his belongings to his friends. On 19 April 1739, he was taken through the streets of York in an open cart to be hanged. He climbed on to the platform in front of a huge crowd. He threw himself off the ladder without any help from the executioner and died in a few minutes.

SOURCE 3

Turpin showed calmness and courage. He talked for some time to the hangman and gave him a small ivory whistle as a gift.

An eyewitness report on what happened when Turpin was hanged.

Activity Time

1 Use the information you have just read to make a six frame storyboard of Turpin's life. Pick six different events. Use drawings and at least one sentence to describe each event.

2 In pairs decide on two events that would have made Turpin famous in his own lifetime.

3 Why is Turpin's story so good that he has been remembered for a long time after his death?

HOW HAS DICK TURPIN BEEN PORTRAYED: GLAMOROUS HIGHWAYMAN OR NASTY VILLAIN?

A lot of the Dick Turpin story is legend. Remember that a legend is a mix of fact and stories that people think are good.

Dick Turpin and Black Bess Ride fact or fiction?

There was another legend about a ride from London to York.

One morning in 1676, a fearless highwayman called John 'Nick' Nevins robbed a sailor in Kent. He needed to escape arrest. So he rode 190 miles in about 15 hours. By eight o'clock that evening he was playing bowls on a green in York. When rumours spread of his amazing ride across England, he became known as 'Swift Nick'.

SOURCE 1

And the highwayman came riding, riding, riding,
The highwayman came riding, up to the old inn door.

He'd a French hat on his forehead, a bunch of lace at his chin,
A coat of red velvet, and trousers of brown deer skin.

Over the cobbles he clattered and clashed in the dark inn-yard,
He tapped with his whip on the shutters, but all was locked and barred,
He whistled a tune to the window, and who should be waiting there
But the landlord's black-eyed daughter,
Bess, landlord's daughter,
Plaiting a dark red love-knot into her long black hair.

A poem by Alfred Noyes written in 1913.

So perhaps it was not Dick Turpin who really made the fast ride to York. Turpin did not become famous for the ride until 100 years after it took place. In 1834 a best-selling novel included a highwayman called Dick Turpin who made a daring journey. Perhaps this is how the legend started.

SOURCE 2

A woodcut done in the 1700s showing Turpin escaping from the authorities.

SOURCE 3

Only at the very end of his life, while waiting to be hanged, did Turpin show any real bravery. Before that his life was unpleasant, to say the least.

A modern historian writing about the behaviour of Dick Turpin just before he was hanged.

Question Time

❶ What sort of image of the highwayman is given in Source 1? Think about:
- what he is wearing
- what he is doing
- what he is carrying
- how other people react towards him.

❷ Look at Source 2. Does it agree with the image of the highwayman given in Source 1? Look at the same points as you did in the last question.

❸ a Go back to your storyboard. For each frame pick a word or phrase that sums up Turpin.
b What view of Turpin's life is shown in your storyboard. Do you make him look like a hero or a thief?
c Do you think that people in the eighteenth century would have seen Turpin more as a hero or a thief? Explain your answer.

WINSTON CHURCHILL

WHO WAS WINSTON CHURCHILL?

Churchill is our third and last individual with a reputation. In a few words, write down why you think Churchill is famous. Compare your ideas with other people in the class. Do you all agree or are there different ideas?

PERSONNEL FILE

Birth	1874 in Blenheim Palace, Oxfordshire. Son of a Lord.
Education	Harrow School and the Royal Military College, Sandhurst.
Marriage	To Clementine Hozier.
Job	Politician, journalist, soldier, author, artist, war leader.
Famous events in life	1898 Churchill fights in Egypt. 1899 He is a newspaper reporter in the Boer War in South Africa. He is captured but escapes.

1900 Churchill becomes a Conservative MP. He swaps to join the Liberal Party, but then rejoins the Conservatives in 1922.

1926 During the General Strike in Britain, Churchill writes for the government newspaper.

1939 At the start of the Second World War Churchill takes over running the Navy.

1940 Churchill becomes Prime Minister in a government made up of all political parties. He leads Britain to win the Second World War. |

PERSONNEL FILE

Continued

1945 He is beaten by the Labour Party in the General Election.

1951 He becomes Prime Minister again.

1955 Churchill retires from government and publishes a set of six books. These win the Nobel Prize for Literature.

Death

1965 On 24 January after several strokes.

Question Time

Think back to what you wrote about Churchill at the start of this section. Had you, or anyone in your class, written about him being anything other than a war-time leader or prime minister?

❶ List the jobs that Churchill held in his lifetime.

❷ Rank these jobs to show which made him most famous. Clue: war-time leader would probably be given position number 1.

LIFE AND WORK UP TO 1938 – WHAT MOTIVATED CHURCHILL?

CHURCHILL'S EARLY LIFE

- He was from a very wealthy family. His father had also been a Conservative MP and his mother was a writer.
- He trained men on the Western Front in the First World War. For part of the war he was in charge of the making of aeroplanes, guns, shells and tanks.

SOURCE 1

Churchill cannot imagine Britain without an empire, or without wars involved to keep an empire. A hundred years ago he might have changed our country's history. But now people believe in peace and equality.

An extract from a book by J. R. Clynes. It was published in 1937.

CHURCHILL AND EMPIRE

Some of Britain's colonies had become independent by the end of the First World War. These included Canada, Australia and South Africa.

In the 1920s and 30s, India also wanted to rule itself. The British government started talks with Indian leaders about independence.

Churchill did not support independence for India or any other **colony**.

CHURCHILL AND COMMUNISM

- In 1917 communists took power from the monarchy in Russia. Led by Lenin, they believed that the Communist Party should rule the country for the workers and the peasants.
- The communists were against some people having more wealth and power than others.
- Not everyone agreed with them. They were opposed by a group called the 'Whites', who wanted to bring back the monarchy.
- Churchill supported the Whites.

CHURCHILL AND THE WORKERS

In 1910 Churchill was Home Secretary in the Liberal government. That year there were lots of strikes by trades unions across Britain. They were protesting about falling wages.

Churchill and the government were against the strikes. On one occasion, there was a riot in a Welsh mining town. Churchill sent in troops to break up the riot. The miners were not happy and criticised Churchill.

Question Time

❶ Look at Source 1 on page 239. Working in pairs, check that you and your partner agree about what J. R. Clynes is saying about Churchill. Discuss your ideas.

❷ How would you sum up Churchill's ideas and beliefs?

What does it mean?

Colony
Land ruled by another country.

In South Wales and the North of England many mines were closing and unemployment was rising. Miners went on strike in 1926 and asked all other workers in trades unions to strike too.

More than two million workers joined the strike, which became known as the General Strike. There were no workers for power stations, trains, buses or shipyards. Britain nearly came to a halt as there were food and power shortages.

Churchill wanted to break the strike. He ran the special newspaper that the government published. It was called the *British Gazette*. Source 2 is from this newspaper. After nine days the strike was called off. The government and Churchill had won.

SOURCE 2

Either the country will break the General Strike or the General Strike will break the country. His Majesty's government will not back down.

From the *British Gazette*, 6 May 1926.

SOURCE 3

Churchill told me that we both wanted the same thing, only we had different ideas of how to get it. He believed that the richer the rich get, the more they are able to help the poor.

Jennie Lee speaking about events in 1926. She became a Labour MP in 1928. She supported policies that took money from the upper class and used it to help the working class.

Question Time

1 What did Churchill think about the British Empire?

2 What did Churchill think of communism?

3 What did Churchill think about the General Strike?

4 Does Churchill's background help us to understand his ideas and beliefs? Discuss this question in small groups.

CHURCHILL AND THE SECOND WORLD WAR

CHURCHILL AND HITLER

In 1938 the situation in Europe was very tense. Hitler was breaking the terms of the Treaty of Versailles made at the end of the First World War, but no one tried to stop him.

In Britain there were two points of view about what should be done about Hitler.

- Prime Minister of Britain, Neville Chamberlain, wanted to give in to Hitler and let him take the Sudetenland, part of Czechoslovakia. The aim was to stop a war. This was called 'Appeasement'. He believed Hitler was just taking back land that was Germany's before the First World War and that he would then be happy. Chamberlain met Hitler at a conference in Munich and agreed to let him have the Sudetenland. Most British people supported Chamberlain as they did not want another war.
- Churchill disagreed with appeasement. He did not trust Hitler and criticised Chamberlain.

Hitler was not happy with just the Sudetenland. He took over the rest of Czechoslovakia and got ready to invade Poland next. Britain and France had promised to help Poland if Germany invaded. When German armies entered Poland on 1 September, Britain declared war two days later.

CHURCHILL AS WAR LEADER

- King George VI asked Churchill to lead a special government made up of all parties. This is called a coalition.
- When Churchill took over, the war was going badly for Britain. It looked as though Germany could not be stopped.
- Britain was the only country left in western Europe that could fight back, so a huge effort was needed.

SOURCE 1

We have been totally beaten. This is not the end, it is only the beginning.

Churchill speaking to MPs after meeting Hitler at Munich in 1938.

SOURCE 2

A poster from 1940.

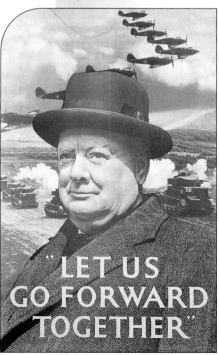

"LET US GO FORWARD TOGETHER"

It was vital to keep the morale (or spirits) of the British public high. This was done using posters like the one shown in Source 2. Churchill also made radio speeches that were heard all over the British empire.

Here are some extracts from speeches made by Churchill. Think about how these words helped to win the war.

Question Time

❶ Look at Source 2. Use the image of Churchill, the background pictures and the words used to explain why this poster was made.

❷ What sort of man and leader does Churchill seem in the poster?

I say to you, I have nothing to offer but blood, toil, tears and sweat.

Speech in Commons, 13 May 1940.

Arm yourselves and be men of courage. Be ready for the fight. It is better to die in battle than to see our nation and our religion beaten.

Churchill's first BBC broadcast as Prime Minister, 19 May 1940.

We shall fight on the beaches. We shall fight in the fields and in the streets. We shall fight in the hills. Will shall never surrender!

Speech to MPs, 4 June 1940.

The gratitude (thanks) of every home in our island, in our empire and indeed in the world goes to the British airmen who are turning the tide of the war. Never before was so much owed by so many to so few.

Speech to MPs, 20 August 1940.

Question Time

1 In his speeches Churchill was trying to get support from the British people. His speeches made them feel certain emotions. He wanted them to feel:

- proud
- determined
- brave
- religious
- patriotic
- willing to make sacrifices for the war.

a Choose three speech extracts from page 243.

b Work out which of the above emotions Churchill was trying to arouse in your three speeches. (There might be more than one emotion for each speech.) You could put your information on a chart like the one below.

	When speech was made	What Churchill made people feel
My first chosen speech		
My second chosen speech		
My third chosen speech		

2 Churchill was not just aiming his speeches at the British public. Who else was he appealing to?

TURNING THE TIDE: GETTING THE USA'S SUPPORT FOR THE WAR

Churchill thought that it was very important to get support from the USA against Germany. The USA was wealthy and powerful. It would make a good ally. However, most Americans were against going to war in Europe. Churchill had to work hard to get their support. Churchill managed to get President Roosevelt to give Britain and the USSR a lot of materials to help in the war.

Activity Time

Use the information on pages 238 to 243 to make a six frame storyboard of Churchill's life to 1945.

Pick six events. Use drawings and sentences to describe what happens in each frame.

HOW HAS CHURCHILL BEEN PORTRAYED?

Look at the people in the cartoon in Source 1. Which one is Winston Churchill?

SOURCE 1

This cartoon was drawn for Churchill's 80th birthday. It shows a room full of many different 'Churchills'. They are all drinking a toast to Sir Winston Churchill who is sitting in his armchair. The cartoon is saying that Churchill has had a long and interesting life, with lots of different roles.

From 1919 to 1962, David Low drew political cartoons for British newspapers. Many of these cartoons were of Churchill and they were not always positive.

Low was from Australia. He wanted independence for nations that were part of the British Empire. This meant that he usually disagreed with Churchill about the British Empire. Why might Low have softened his attitude towards Churchill in this cartoon?

In 1939 Churchill became the star of many of Low's cartoons. Low also disagreed with appeasement and was very anti-Hitler, even though most people agreed with Chamberlain (see page 242).

During the war Low supported Churchill with cartoons like the one in Source 2 and slogans like 'We're all behind you, Winston!' He often drew Churchill as the only man who could save Britain from Hitler.

This was very different to earlier when Low had made fun of Churchill's ideas. Low was not the only person to change his mind about Churchill, as Source 3 shows.

SOURCE 3

I then (1926) thought he was the most dangerous of all politicians. He was brilliant. But he had foolish and old-fashioned views. It is surprising that I was to become his admirer in the later thirties.

Kingsley Martin, writing in 1966 about Churchill.

SOURCE 2

A cartoon of Churchill, by David Low. It was shown in the *Evening Standard*, a London newspaper.

Question Time

❶ Look at Source 2.
a What is the slogan referring to?
b What sort of man does Churchill seem to be?

❷ Look at Source 1. Can you spot any versions of Churchill that Low would have not liked?

❸ What did Churchill do in 1926 that would explain why Kingsley Martin thought he was so dangerous?

❹ What did Churchill do to make people like Low and Martin change their minds about him in the late-1930s?

WAS CHURCHILL'S IMPACT FOR 'GOOD' OR 'ILL'?

Activity Time

❶ Draw two spider diagrams:
- one with 'good' at the centre, and
- the other with 'bad'.

Fill your spider diagrams with ideas about Churchill. Include:
- things he was good/bad at, and
- how he helped/held back Britain and the world in his lifetime.

❷ Write an obituary of Churchill. (An obituary is written just after someone's death. It describes their life and what they have achieved.) You could use the headings from the Personnel File on page 238 to help you , but you will need to add a headline. You could also use these phrases to help you start writing some of the sections. But you will need to put them in a logical order.

- *Churchill was not only a great politician ...*
- *He had a privileged childhood ...*
- *Churchill was a clever and skilful man. He had many different jobs, starting with ...*
- *Sir Winston Churchill died today, at the age of ...*
- *He was most popular in ... when ...*
- *Churchill had not always been so popular, for example ...*

❸ How would Churchill's obituary have been different if he had died in 1939. Discuss in pairs what the difference would be in the obituary and the headline that would have been used.

Index